SPANISH IN YOUR FACE!

The only book to match 1,001 smiles, frowns, and gestures to Spanish expressions so you can learn to live the language!

LUC NISSET • MARY McVEY GILL

Mc
Graw
Hill

New York Chicago San Francisco Lisbon London Madrid Mexico City
Milan New Delhi San Juan Seoul Singapore Sydney Toronto

Library of Congress Cataloging-in-Publication Data

Nisset, Luc.
    Spanish in your face! : the only book to match 1,001 smiles, frowns, and gestures to Spanish expressions so you can learn to live the language! / Luc Nisset ; with Mary McVey Gill.
        p.   cm.
    Includes index.
    ISBN 0-07-143297-3 (alk. paper)
    1. Nonverbal communication.   2. Spanish language—Terms and phrases.   3. Spanish language—Idioms.   I. Gill, Mary McVey.   II. Title.

P99.5.N55   2007
302.2'22—dc22   2007029505

Thanks to Myriam Castillo for her many suggestions and invaluable linguistic advice throughout the project.   —*Mary McVey Gill*

1 2 3 4 5 6 7 8 9 0 DOC/DOC 0 9 8 7

ISBN-13: 978-0-07-143297-9
ISBN-10:   0-07-143297-3

All illustrations by Luc Nisset
Interior design by Village Typographers, Inc.

Also in this series: French in Your Face!

Also illustrated by Luc Nisset:
    101 French Idioms
    101 French Proverbs
    101 Spanish Idioms
    101 Spanish Proverbs
    101 Spanish Riddles

McGraw-Hill books are available at special quantity discounts to use as premiums and sales promotions, or for use in corporate training programs. For more information, please write to the Director of Special Sales, Professional Publishing, McGraw-Hill, Two Penn Plaza, New York, NY 10121-2298. Or contact your local bookstore.

This book is printed on acid-free paper.

contents

"pre-face"   v

character and personality   1

polar opposites   2

Personalidatos   38

personality types A–Z   41

moods, emotions, and attitudes   73

mood swings   74

Humorómetro   92

emotions and attitudes A–Z   95

appearance and gestures   119

facial descriptions   120

la agencia de contactos   132

body language   134

english-spanish index   151

spanish-english index   153

"pre-face"

Let's face it: A face is worth a thousand words. It can reveal our character and signal our emotions and moods—even when we attempt to hide our feelings. You sometimes expect people to know how you feel just by looking at your face. The messages that faces express are an essential ingredient of human interaction. When we communicate in another language, it is important to notice and understand the facial expressions of the native speaker we are talking to.

Spanish in Your Face! is designed to open up your receptivity to nonverbal communication. It links Spanish terms, common expressions, idioms, and colloquialisms to the character, personality, mood, facial appearance, and gestures that lie behind them. Learning or enriching your knowledge of a language should be a rewarding source of pleasure. We hope you find this book and its illustrations to be amusing and, as the title suggests, *in your face!*

using this book

Just have fun! You can browse through the book, pausing where an illustration grabs your attention, or you can look up specific emotions or moods in either the index or the detailed contents at the beginning of each unit. You can also take the lighthearted quizzes in each unit to pinpoint areas to focus on. Whichever way you use this book, enjoy it. It will enrich your Spanish!

Spanish in Your Face! has many unique features:

- Each of the 108 key terms in the first two units is accompanied by an illustration designed to provide context, reinforce meaning, and aid learning.

- Captions provide English translations for the speech bubbles in the first unit and in the *gestures* section.

- Words that are synonymous or similar to each headword are listed, including adjectives, nouns, and verbs. Many of these are cognates or near-cognates of the English words, making them easier to learn.

- Related terms and expressions are listed to provide additional everyday vocabulary and commonly used phrases.

- Opposites are listed for some headwords. Note that in the sections *polar opposites* and *mood swings,* contrasting character types and emotions appear on facing pages.

- The symbol ◑ indicates colloquial terms or slang expressions that are somewhat off-color and should be used only in appropriate situations.

- Feminine forms and endings are indicated in parentheses. The **tú** form is generally used rather than **usted** for *you.*

- For words, phrases, and expressions that are geographically restricted, the country or region of use is indicated in square brackets.

abbreviations of grammatical terms

adj	adjective
colloq.	colloquial
f	feminine
fpl	feminine plural
lit.	literally
m	masculine
m/f	masculine or feminine
mpl	masculine plural

identification of countries and regions

Arg	Argentina
Bol	Bolivia
C Am	Central America
Carib	Caribbean
Chile	Chile
Col	Colombia
CR	Costa Rica
Cuba	Cuba
Ec	Ecuador
El Salv	El Salvador
L Am	Latin America
Mex	Mexico
Nic	Nicaragua
Peru	Peru
S Am	South America
S Cone	Southern Cone (Argentina, Uruguay, Paraguay)
Spain	Spain
Ven	Venezuela

character and personality

polar opposites

2 decisive ~ indecisive 3
4 enthusiastic ~ killjoy 5
6 erudite ~ ignorant 7
8 focused ~ distracted 9
10 generous ~ stingy 11
12 helpful ~ indifferent 13
14 mature ~ immature 15
16 modest ~ show-off 17
18 nice ~ mean 19
20 optimistic ~ pessimistic 21
22 polite ~ rude 23
24 profound ~ superficial 25
26 relaxed ~ stiff 27
28 reserved ~ talkative 29
30 self-confident ~ unsure of oneself 31
32 sociable ~ unsociable 33
34 well-organized ~ disorganized 35
36 workaholic ~ lazy 37

Personalidatos 38

personality types
A–Z

affectionate 41
aggressive 42
boring 43
clumsy 44
crafty 45
crazy 46
distrustful 47
dogmatic 48
eccentric 49
gossipy 50
honest 51
hypocritical 52
indecent 53
insignificant 54
intermediary 55
kindly 56
leader 57
life of the party 58
loser 59
melodramatic 60
obliging 61
peacemaker 62
pretentious 63
prosperous 64
reliable 65
respectful 66
romantic 67
star 68
uncomfortable 69
well-informed 70
wolf 71

Personalidatos RESULTS 72

decisive decidido(-a)

Let's go!
¡Vámonos!

That's how we'll leave it. (lit., *We remain this way.*)
Así quedamos.

I'm sure.
Estoy seguro.

There's no turning back. (lit., *There's no turning of the page.*)
No hay vuelta de hoja.

I've decided.
Ya lo he decidido.

I'm determined to do it.
Estoy resuelto a hacerlo.

synonyms and similar words

cabezón (cabezona) pigheaded
cierto(-a) certain
determinado(-a) determined
firme firm
obstinado(-a) obstinate
porfiado(-a) obstinate

resuelto(-a) resolute
seguro(-a) confident, sure
tenaz tenacious
terco(-a) stubborn
testarudo(-a) headstrong, stubborn
tozudo(-a) stubborn

related terms and expressions

Agarró el toro por las astas.	He grabbed the bull by the horns.
Agarró el toro por los cuernos.	He grabbed the bull by the horns.
Él no se raja.	He doesn't back down. (*colloq.*)
Lo hizo sin titubeos.	He did it without hesitation.
No va a cambiar de opinión.	She won't change her mind.
Quemó las naves.	He burned his bridges (*lit.*, ships).
Sale y vale. Trato hecho.	Agreed. It's a done deal.
Se mantiene en sus trece.	He sticks to his guns (*lit.*, stays in his thirteen).
Tiene mucha confianza en sí mismo(-a).	He/She has a lot of confidence in himself/herself.
Tomó una decisión.	She made a decision.
Va a terminar este proyecto, cueste lo que cueste.	She'll do whatever it takes to finish this project.

I'm not sure. No estoy seguro.

No puedo decidir. *I can't decide.*

I'm on the fence (lit., *between two waters*). Estoy entre dos aguas.

Tengo mis dudas. *I have my doubts.*

Estoy vacilando. *I'm hesitant.*

synonyms and similar words

caprichoso(-a) impulsive, given to following whims
confundido(-a) confused
desorientado(-a) disoriented
incierto(-a) uncertain, unsure
inconstante changing, inconstant
perplejo(-a) bewildered, baffled
vacilante hesitant

related terms and expressions

Cambia de ideas como de pantalones.	He changes ideas as often as he changes pants.
Es un(a) derrotista.	He's/She's a quitter.
No sé con qué carta quedarme.	I don't know what to do (*lit.*, which card to keep).
Quien pestañea pierde.	He who hesitates is lost. (*lit.*, He who blinks loses.)
Vaya uno a saber.	Go figure. / Who knows?

entre la espada y la pared between a rock and a hard place (*lit.*, the sword and the wall)

pesar los pros y los contras to weigh the pros and cons
titubear to waver
vacilar to hesitate

It's the best!

Wonderful!

I love it!

¡Súper!

¡Me encanta!

¡Es lo máximo!

¡Es un verdadero aficionado!

¡Le entusiasma todo!

He's a real fan!

He's enthusiastic about everything!

synonyms and similar words

afanoso(-a) eager
apasionado(-a) passionate
ardiente ardent
deseoso(-a) eager
dinámico(-a) dynamic
emocionado(-a) thrilled, excited
enardecido(-a) fired up
encantado(-a) delighted

fanático(-a) fanatical
fascinado(-a) fascinated
ferviente devoted, fervent
frenético(-a) frantic
impetuoso(-a) impetuous
loco(-a) por crazy about
poseído(-a) possessed
vehemente vehement

related terms and expressions

¡Qué entusiasmo!   What enthusiasm!

adorar to adore, love
anhelar mucho to be eager/zealous
enardecerse to get fired up
exaltarse to get worked up / excited

con la camiseta puesta all fired up, as a real enthusiast
  (*lit.,* with his or her T-shirt on)

admirador(a) *m/f* admirer
aficionado(-a) *m/f* fan
discípulo(-a) *m/f* disciple, follower
hincha *m/f* fan (sports)

Another party where people are acting like fools.

How boring!

I won't go!

Otra fiesta de locos.

¡Qué aburrido!

No iré.

Pero Juana, ¡es TU fiesta de cumpleaños!

Tendrás que ir. ¡No seas aguafiestas!

But, Juana, it's YOUR birthday party!

You have to go. Don't be a party pooper!

synonyms and similar words

crítico(-a) critical
deprimido(-a) depressed
descontento(-a) unhappy
despectivo(-a) disparaging, pejorative

destructivo(-a) destructive
pesimista pessimistic
triste sad

related terms and expressions

El gozo en un pozo. (REFRÁN)

¡Qué tristeza!

arruinar to ruin
criticar to criticize
denigrar to denigrate
desanimar to discourage
desaprobar to disapprove
desilusionar to disillusion
despreciar to disparage, disdain, put down
echar la culpa to blame
juzgar to judge
mantenerse de mal genio to be bad-tempered
matar la alegría to kill (others') joy

It's all down the drain. (*lit.*, The pleasure in a well.)
How pathetic!

reparar en migajas to split hairs (*lit.*, to notice crumbs)
ser sangrón (sangrona) to be unpleasant/boring/annoying (*colloq.*) [Mex, C Am, Carib]
ser un(a) criticón (criticona) to be a Negative Nelly (always critical)
ser un(a) reparón (reparona) to be a hairsplitter (always finding fault)
subestimar to underestimate
tener mala leche to be grumpy/ unpleasant (*lit.*, to have bad milk) (*colloq.*)

A computer doesn't cultivate your intelligence.

It's curiosity and the desire to know.

No es la computadora que cultiva tu inteligencia.

Es la curiosidad y el deseo de saber.

Nosotros queremos saberlo todo, abuela.

We wanna know everything, Grandma.

Antes que todo, ¿dónde están las chocolatinas que nos prometiste?

And first of all, where are the chocolates you promised us?

synonyms and similar words

avispado(-a) sharp (*colloq.*)
culto(-a) cultured
experto(-a) expert
instruido(-a) well-educated

inteligente intelligent
letrado(-a) learned
sabio(-a) wise
superdotado(-a) very gifted

related terms and expressions

Ella es un coco.
She's a brain (*lit.*, coconut). (*colloq.*) [L Am]

Ella tiene mucho coco.
She's a brain (*lit.*, has a lot of coconut). (*colloq.*) [Spain]

Es un cerebro, un genio.
He's a brain, a genius.

Es una enciclopedia andando.
She's a walking encyclopedia.

Lo conoce como la palma de la mano.
He knows it like the palm of his hand.

Lo sabe al dedillo.
She knows it to a "T." / She has the knowledge at her fingertips.

Se va a empapar en literatura rusa. Es una mujer de letras.
She's going to steep herself in / bone up on Russian literature. She's a well-educated woman.

Vale más saber que tener.
(REFRÁN)
It's better to know (things) than to have (things).

Um ...

I don't know.

Moron.

What an illiterate!

Fool!

How could I have married this ignoramus?

synonyms and similar words

analfabeta illiterate
baboso(-a) stupid, foolish
bruto(-a) brutish, stupid
casquivano(-a) scatterbrained
estúpido(-a) extremely stupid
　(*stronger than English*)
grosero(-a) rude, crude
iletrado(-a) illiterate

inculto(-a) uneducated
lelo(-a) foolish, stupid [parts of L Am]
menso(-a) foolish, stupid [L Am]
nulo(-a) useless, stupid
pasmado(-a) dumb, stupid [Mex, C Am]
primitivo(-a) primitive
zonzo(-a) foolish, stupid [most of L Am]

related terms and expressions

no tener dos dedos de frente to have less sense than God gave a goose
　(*lit.,* to not have two fingers' (width) of forehead)
ser un pedazo de alcornoque to be a blockhead (*lit.,* piece of cork oak)
tener la cabeza hueca to be an airhead

boludo(-a) *m/f* moron, asshole
　[S Cone]
burro(-a) *m/f* donkey, ass
cabeza *f* **de chorlito** birdbrain
cabeza *f* **de mosquito** birdbrain
　[Spain, S Cone]
cretino(-a) *m/f* idiot
gil(a) *m/f* dunce, chump [L Am]

gilipollas *m/f* moron, asshole [Spain]
pendejo(-a) *m/f* moron, asshole
　[most of L Am, not S Cone]
tonto(-a) *m/f* **de capirote** complete
　idiot (*lit.,* idiot chief)
tonto(-a) *m/f* **perdido(-a)** complete
　idiot (*lit.,* lost idiot)

focused | concentrado(-a)

What concentration! Suddenly the winning lottery numbers came to him.

¡Qué concentración! De súbito se le vinieron a su mente los números ganadores de la lotería.

Eso te hace pensar.

It makes you think.

synonyms and similar words

absorto(-a) absorbed
atento(-a) attentive
centrado(-a) centered, focused
enfocado(-a) focused
introspectivo(-a) introspective
meditativo(-a) meditative
observador(a) observant
pensativo(-a) pensive, thoughtful
reflexivo(-a) reflective, thoughtful
vigilante vigilant

related terms and expressions

abstraerse to be lost in thought
consultar con la almohada to sleep on it, think about something overnight (*lit.,* to consult with the pillow)
ensimismarse to become engrossed
estar absorto(-a) en sus recuerdos to be absorbed in one's memories
estar perdido(-a) en sus pensamientos to be lost in his/her thoughts
reflexionar sobre un problema to reflect on a problem
ser despierto(-a) to be alert/sharp

What a scatterbrain! — ¡Qué despistado!

I lose everything! — ¡Todo lo pierdo!

I forgot my wallet! — ¡Se me olvidó la billetera!

How forgetful! — ¡Qué olvidadizo!

I'm very disorganized. — Soy muy desorganizado.

synonyms and similar words

atolondrado(-a) thoughtless, scatterbrained
desatento(-a) inattentive
descuidado(-a) careless
desorganizado(-a) disorganized

despistado(-a) clueless, scatterbrained
incauto(-a) unwary, gullible
negligente negligent
olvidadizo(-a) forgetful
soñador(a) spacy, dreamy

related terms and expressions

Desconecté.	I tuned out.
Está en la luna.	He's daydreaming (*lit.*, on the moon).
Está en las nubes.	She has her head in the clouds.
Está más despistado que un pulpo en un garaje.	He's clueless (*lit.*, more lost than an octopus in a garage).
Está perdido en sus pensamientos.	He's lost in his thoughts.
Estoy como una regadera.	My mind is like a sieve. [Spain]
Estoy fuera de onda.	I'm out of it.
Por un oído le entra y por el otro le sale.	It goes in one ear and out the other.
¡Qué cabeza de chorlito!	What a birdbrain!
Se me olvidó por completo.	It completely slipped my mind.
Si no tuviera la cabeza pegada al cuerpo, la perdería.	If I didn't have my head attached to my body, I'd lose it.
Tengo la mente en blanco.	My mind is blank.

generous | generoso(-a)

She is good as gold (lit., bread); she gives without thinking of being compensated.

Ella es buena como el pan; da sin pensar en recompensas.

Tiene un corazón de oro.

She has a heart of gold.

synonyms and similar words

abnegado(-a) self-sacrificing
altruista altruistic
benévolo(-a) benevolent
bondadoso(-a) kind
bueno(-a) good
caritativo(-a) charitable
desinteresado(-a) selfless, unselfish

espléndido(-a) generous, lavish
humano(-a) humane, understanding
magnánimo(-a) magnanimous
munífico(-a) munificent, giving
regalador(a) gift-giving

related terms and expressions

Haz el bien y no mires a quien. (REFRÁN)
Do good deeds to everyone. (*lit.*, Do good and don't look to whom.)

Le gusta convidar.
He likes to invite/treat others.

Les da a los pobres, los menos afortunados.
She gives to the poor, the less fortunate.

Tiene buen corazón.
She's good-hearted.

dar hasta la camisa con tal de ayudarle a alguien to give the shirt off one's back to help someone

benefactor(a) *m/f* benefactor
filántropo(-a) *m/f* philanthropist
mecenas *m* sponsor, patron
santo(-a) *m/f* saint

That tightwad left me hardly any tip.

Ese agarrado me dejó muy poca propina.

Algunos clientes son muy tacaños.

¡Qué codo eres! La propina debe ser de un quince por ciento.

Some customers are really stingy.

What a cheapskate you are! The tip is supposed to be 15%.

But the fish wasn't very fresh.

Pero el pescado no estaba muy fresco.

synonyms and similar words

agarrado(-a) tightfisted
ahorrador(a) thrifty
amarrado(-a) stingy
apretado(-a) tightfisted [L Am]
avaro(-a) miserly
codicioso(-a) greedy, covetous

cutre cheap [Spain]
interesado(-a) selfish, self-interested
mezquino(-a) stingy
miserable miserly, wretched
parsimonioso(-a) parsimonious

related terms and expressions

Gatos y niños siempre dicen "Mío, mío, mío." (REFRÁN)   Cats and children always say "Mine, mine, mine" ("Meow, meow, meow").

apretarse el cinturón to tighten one's belt

no comer un huevo por no perder la cáscara to be stingy/miserly (*lit.,* to not eat an egg so as not to waste the shell)

no dar ni la hora to be stingy (*lit.,* to not give even the time of day)

no dar ni los "buenos días" to be stingy (*lit.,* to not give even a "Good day")

ser codo(-a) to be a cheapskate (*lit.,* to be elbow) [Mex, C Am, Carib]

más agarrado(-a) que la hiedra de la roca tighter/stingier than ivy on a rock

◑ **tan amarrado(-a) que no da ni del cuerpo** so tight he/she doesn't even go to the bathroom

amarrete *m/f* tightwad [S Am]

synonyms and similar words

altruista altruistic	**cariñoso(-a)** affectionate
atento(-a) attentive	**caritativo(-a)** charitable, kind
benévolo(-a) benevolent	**complaciente** obliging, accommodating
bondadoso(-a) kind	**desinteresado(-a)** unselfish
caballeroso gentlemanly	**solícito(-a)** solicitous, obliging

related terms and expressions

¡Auxilio! / ¡Socorro!	Help!
El acomedido come de lo que está escondido. (REFRÁN)	Helping out others will pay off. (*lit.,* The volunteer eats what is hidden.)
Eso está hecho.	Consider it done. [Spain]
Estoy a sus órdenes.	I'm at your service.

acomedirse to volunteer [L Am]

darle/echarle una mano a alguien to give someone a hand

ir al rescate to go to the rescue

meter las manos al fuego por alguien to vouch for someone (*lit.,* to put one's hands to the fire for someone)

ofrecerse para hacer algo to volunteer to do something

palanquear to push buttons (*lit.,* move levers) to help someone [S Am]

sacar a alguien de un apuro to get someone out of a jam

sacar la cara por alguien to go to bat for someone (*lit.,* to take off one's face for someone)

It doesn't interest me in the least.

No me interesa en lo más mínimo.

¡Egoísta!

Todo le resbala.

How selfish!

Everything rolls off his back.

It's all the same to me.

I couldn't care less. (lit., It matters a cucumber to me.)

Me da igual.

Me importa un pepino.

Se ríe de los peces de colores.

He lets it roll off his back. (lit., He laughs at colored fish.)

synonyms and similar words

apático(-a) apathetic	**impasible** impassive
duro(-a) hard	**imperturbable** imperturbable
egoísta selfish	**insensible** insensitive
estoico(-a) stoic	**sin corazón** heartless

related terms and expressions

Es un(a) pasota; pasa de todo.	He/She is a slacker; he/she doesn't care about anything. [Spain]
Llueva o truene es igual.	It's all the same. (*lit.*, Whether it rains or thunders, it's the same.)
Me importa lo mismo ocho que ochenta.	It's the same to me. (*lit.*, Eight matters to me as much as eighty.)
⊙ **Me importan tres cojones.**	I don't give a damn. (*lit.*, It's as important to me as three testicles.) [Spain]
⊙ **Me la suda.**	I don't give a damn.
⊙ **Me vale madre.**	I don't give a damn. [Mex, C Am]
No me hace ni fu ni fa.	I could take it or leave it. (*lit.*, It doesn't do fu or fa for me.)
¿Qué más da?	Who cares? (*lit.*, What more does it give?) [L Am]
⊙ **valemadrismo** *m* slacker attitude [Mex]	

mature | maduro(-a)

I've got news for you: From now on, you have to grow up.

Les tengo una noticia: de ahora en adelante, tendrán que madurar.

Quiero ver mutuo respeto y comprensión entre ustedes dos.

¡El primero que hable de divorcio se las tendrá que ver conmigo!

I want to see mutual respect and understanding between you.

The first one who brings up divorce will have to deal with me!

synonyms and similar words

adulto(-a) adult
juicioso(-a) judicious, wise
precoz precocious
prudente prudent

razonable reasonable
responsable responsible
sensato(-a) sensible
serio(-a) serious

related terms and expressions

Es maduro(-a) para su edad.
Es un hombre hecho y derecho
 (una mujer hecha y derecha).
Es un niño (una niña) prodigio.
Más sabe el diablo por ser viejo
 que por ser diablo. (REFRÁN)

He's/She's mature for his/her age.
He's/She's a grown (*lit.*, made and
 upright) man/woman.
He's/She's a child prodigy.
The devil knows more because he's
 old (and experienced) than because
 he's the devil.

circunspección *f* circumspection
cordura *f* common sense
discernimiento *m* judgment
inteligencia *f* intelligence
madurez *f* maturity
mesura *f* moderation, restraint
prudencia *f* caution, prudence
razón *f* reason

Skip the math class! Bambi's playing downtown.

¡Olvídate de la clase de matemáticas! Ahora están presentando Bambi en el centro.

Shall we go?

¿Vamos?

Hombre, ¡madura un poco!

Grow up, dude!

Te sigues portando como un niño.

You still act like a child.

Parece que todavía estás en pañales.

Looks like you're still wet behind the ears (lit., in diapers).

synonyms and similar words

adolescente teenaged, adolescent
aniñado(-a) childish, childlike
infantil infantile, childish
ingenuo(-a) ingenuous, naive
inocente innocent
irresponsable irresponsible
joven young
juvenil youthful, young, juvenile
pueril puerile, childish

related terms and expressions

Es una fresa. She's a princess (*lit.*, strawberry; implies someone innocent and a bit spoiled).
Está en pañales. He's wet behind the ears (*lit.*, in diapers).
Está muy verde. She's young and inexperienced (*lit.*, green).

chiquillo(-a) *m/f* kid
chiquitín (chiquitina) *m/f* kid
mocoso(-a) *m/f* kid; *adj* snot-nosed
nene (nena) *m/f* kid (*from* **niño(-a)**)

modest | modesto(-a)

I know my place.

I keep a low profile (lit., *try to be invisible*).

I don't like to act presumptuous.

I don't like to call attention to myself.

I'm modest and discreet in everything.

synonyms and similar words

decente decent
discreto(-a) discreet
humilde humble
pudoroso(-a) prudish, modest
recatado(-a) reserved, modest
reservado(-a) reserved
simple plain, simple
sobrio(-a) serious, without excess

related terms and expressions

Es muy hogareña.	She's very devoted to her home.
Es una persona sin ínfulas, sin pretensiones.	She's a person who doesn't put on airs, isn't pretentious.
No es engreída.	She's not stuck-up.
No le gusta hacer teatro.	He doesn't like to make a scene.
No le gusta llamar la atención.	She doesn't like to call attention to herself.
No le gusta usar ropa llamativa.	She doesn't like to wear loud clothing.
sin ceremonia without fanfare	

I just acquired two large properties downtown.

Acabo de adquirir dos grandes propiedades en el centro.

Este tipo... se las da de gran propietario.

Sí, le gusta fanfarronear.

This guy ... he puts on airs of being a big property owner.

Yeah, he likes to toot his own horn.

synonyms and similar words

arrogante arrogant
creído(-a) stuck-up
engreído(-a) stuck-up
estirado(-a) stuck-up [Spain, L Am except Mex]
extrovertido(-a) extroverted
fanfarrón (fanfarrona) braggart
fantasioso(-a) stuck-up; prone to exaggerating

fufurufo(-a) stuck-up [most of L Am]
jactancioso(-a) boastful
orgulloso(-a) proud
presumido(-a) conceited, presumptuous
soberbio(-a) proud
vanidoso(-a) vain

related terms and expressions

Le gusta hacer teatro. She likes to put on a show.
Le gusta pavonearse. He likes to strut around like a peacock.
Se cree el pez gordo. He thinks he's a big shot (*lit.*, the fat fish).
Se da mucha coba. He toots his own horn (*lit.*, gives himself a lot of flattery).

con sus grandes ínfulas with his big-shot attitude (*lit.*, big airs)

alardearse to toot one's own horn
fantochear to show off, toot one's own horn
fardar (de) to act presumptuous, boast or sport (something) [Spain]
jactarse to brag
presumir to act presumptuous

Hi, everyone.

Buenos días, señores.

Llámenme si me necesitan.

Call if you need me!

You can count on me.

Cuenten conmigo.

synonyms and similar words

adorable adorable
agradable pleasant, nice
amable likeable, friendly
amoroso(-a) loving
atento(-a) attentive
bondadoso(-a) kind

cariñoso(-a) affectionate
considerado(-a) considerate
cortés polite, courteous
dulce sweet
generoso(-a) generous
sincero(-a) sincere

related terms and expressions

A todo el mundo le cae bien.	Everyone likes him/her.
Es de pura cepa.	She's the real thing (*lit.*, of pure stock).
Es muy buena gente.	He's very nice.
Es muy buena onda.	She's cool. / She's good. (*colloq.*)
Es un ángel.	She's an angel.
Es un buen tío.	He's a good guy. [Spain]
Es un buen tipo.	He's a good guy.
Es una chica muy amable.	She's a really nice gal.
Es una joya.	He's/She's a gem.
Es una tía muy amable.	She's a nice gal. [Spain]

How awful!

Disgusting!

Ignoramus!

¡Qué barbaridad!

¡Asqueroso!

¡Qué cruel es!

¡Pobre animalito!

¡Bruto!

How cruel he is!

Poor little thing!

synonyms and similar words

agresivo(-a) aggressive
brutal brutal
con corazón de acero hardhearted
 (*lit.*, with a heart of steel)
duro(-a) callous, hardhearted
feroz fierce, ferocious
malicioso(-a) malicious
malintencionado(-a) ill-intentioned

manipulador(a) manipulative
odioso(-a) hateful
perverso(-a) wicked, perverse
rencoroso(-a) spiteful
sádico(-a) sadistic
salvaje savage
sin corazón heartless
vicioso(-a) vicious

related terms and expressions

Es muy sangrón (sangrona).	He/She is a pain/drag. [Mex, C Am, Carib]
Es un(a) canalla.	He/She is a creep.
Es un(a) descarado(-a).	He/She is a scoundrel (*lit.*, someone who doesn't show his or her face).
Me dio mucha lata.	She really gave me a hard time (*lit.*, a lot of tin can).
¡Qué cabronada!	What a damn cheap shot!
¡Qué cagada!	What a crappy cheap shot!
¡Qué mala pasada! / ¡Qué trastada!	What a dirty trick!
¡Qué putada!	What a hell of a thing to do!
cabrón *m/f* bastard	**hijo** *m* **de puta** bastard
cabrona/perra/puta *f* bitch	

She always looks on the bright side.

Siempre ve el lado positivo de las cosas.

¡Dice que todo saldrá bien!

Ella no le teme al futuro.

She says everything will turn out fine!

She has no fear of the future.

Of course, we're going to make progress.

Por supuesto que vamos a salir adelante.

Todo anda sobre ruedas.

Everything is going great.

synonyms and similar words

alentador(a) encouraging
consolador(a) consoling
contento(-a) glad, happy
dinámico(-a) dynamic

positivo(-a) positive
seguro(-a) confident, sure
tranquilizador(a) reassuring

related terms and expressions

Ese arroz ya se coció. (REFRÁN)   It's in the bag. (*lit.*, That rice is already cooked.) [Mex, El Salv]

Tengo fe que todo saldrá bien.   I have faith that everything will turn out well.

Todo anda sobre ruedas.   Everything is going great (*lit.*, on wheels).
Todo marcha requetebién.   Everything is going super.
Todo va viento en popa.   Everything is going great (*lit.*, with the wind at the stern).

alentar to encourage
animar to encourage, cheer/brighten up
creer en su estrella to believe in your lucky star
dar alas to encourage (*lit.*, give wings)
dar ánimo to encourage

dar confianza to reassure, give confidence
entusiasmar to fill with enthusiasm
esperanzar to give hope
ilusionar to build up hopes
verlo todo color de rosa to see life through rose-colored glasses

synonyms and similar words

alarmista alarmist, raising alarms
amargado(-a) bitter
catastrofista predicting catastrophe
cínico(-a) cynical
deprimido(-a) depressed
derrotista defeatist
desconsolado(-a) disconsolate, inconsolable

desilusionado(-a) disillusioned
irascible irascible, bad-tempered
irritable irritable, cantankerous
malhumorado(-a) crabby
melancólico(-a) sad, melancholic
negativo(-a) negative
preocupado(-a) worried
sombrío(-a) somber, serious

related terms and expressions

¿Adónde vamos a parar? — Where are we going to end up?

"El optimista ve una oportunidad en cada calamidad y el pesimista ve una calamidad en cada oportunidad." (Miguel Ángel Cornejo) — "The optimist sees an opportunity in every calamity, and the pessimist sees a calamity in every opportunity."

Es un mal augurio. — It's a bad omen.

¡Qué bajón! — What a bummer!

Se me cayó el alma a los pies. — I lost heart. (*lit.*, My soul fell to my feet.)

Teme lo peor. — She fears the worst.

Tiene una depre. — He's got the blues (*lit.*, has depression).

This young man has good manners.

Este joven tiene buenos modales.

Es muy educado.

Un verdadero modelo.

He's been very well brought up.

A real model (of courtesy).

Always so proper and so polite.

Siempre tan correcto y tan cortés.

synonyms and similar words

afable good-natured
atento(-a) attentive
bien educado(-a) well brought up
caballeroso gentlemanly

correcto(-a) appropriate, proper
culto(-a) educated, cultured
distinguido(-a) distinguished
refinado(-a) refined

related terms and expressions

Con permiso. Excuse me. (*lit.,* With your permission.) (*used when withdrawing from a conversation, stepping in front of someone, etc.*)

Disculpe (usted). Excuse me (for something I've done).
Perdón. Excuse me (for something I've done).

portarse bien to behave oneself
ser de buen gusto to be in good taste

buena educación *f* good upbringing
buenos modales *mpl* good manners
cortesía *f* courtesy
decoro *m* decorum
galantería *f* gallantry
protocolo *m* protocol, etiquette, formality
refinamiento *m* refinement
urbanidad *f* civility

What bad manners!

What a lowlife!

He doesn't care if he walks all over everyone.

What a horrible way to act! (lit., *What horrible behavior!*)

What a rude person!

It looks like no one has taught you the rules of etiquette.

He acts like he's the center of the universe.

synonyms and similar words

borde bad-mannered, rude [Spain]
cafre boorish, rude [Spain]
desatento(-a) inattentive
descarado(-a) shameless
desconsiderado(-a) inconsiderate
grosero(-a) rude, crude
impertinente impertinent
imprudente imprudent

incorrecto(-a) improper
inculto(-a) unrefined, uneducated
insolente insolent
mal educado(-a) rude, badly brought up
malcriado(-a) ill-mannered
ofensivo(-a) insulting, offensive
tosco(-a) rough, unrefined

related terms and expressions

criado(-a) a puro machete brought up in a barn, raised by wolves (*lit.,* raised by machete) [Mex, parts of C Am]

bestia *m/f* lout
bruto(-a) *m/f* lout, brute
grosería *f* vulgarity
insulto *m* insult
lépero(-a) *m/f* coarse, rude person [Mex, C Am]
palabrota *f* bad word
patán *m* lout, lowlife
sinvergüenza *m/f* jerk, shameless person

I came to see you 20 years ago and you told me, "Life is a long, tranquil river."

Hace veinte años vine a verlo y me dijo "La vida es como un río largo y tranquilo."

Eso todavía es verdad; claro, está un poco mejor debido a las conexiones rápidas de Internet.

That's still true; of course, it's a little better with a fast Internet connection.

synonyms and similar words

astuto(-a) astute
avispado(-a) sharp, smart
despejado(-a) alert, not needing sleep
despierto(-a) alert (*with* **ser**)
espabilado(-a) alert, aware, on the ball
gran/grande great, excellent
grave serious
ingenioso(-a) ingenious, clever
insondable deep

inteligente intelligent
intenso(-a) intense
intuitivo(-a) intuitive
lúcido(-a) lucid, clearheaded
penetrante penetrating
perspicaz perceptive
sabio(-a) wise
sagaz shrewd, astute

related terms and expressions

Es demasiado profundo para mí. It's too deep for me.
Es la madre del cordero. It's the heart of the matter (*lit.*, the mother of the lamb).
Es más listo(-a) que el hambre. He's/She's sharp as a tack (*lit.*, sharper than hunger).
Va al fondo de las cosas. He goes deep to the heart of things.

agudeza *f* astuteness, sharpness
discernimiento *m* discernment, insight
inteligencia *f* intelligence
juicio *m* judgment
perspicacia *f* perceptiveness

profundas reflexiones *fpl* deep thinking
sagacidad *f* shrewdness, astuteness
visión *f* vision

Off to the hairdresser again? Didn't you go there this morning?

¿Vas al salón de belleza otra vez? ¿Acaso no fuiste esta mañana?

Voy a ver a otra estilista para que me dé una segunda opinión. ¡No estoy segura si me gusta este permanente!

I'm going to see another stylist to get a second opinion. I'm not sure if I like this perm!

synonyms and similar words

bobo(-a) silly
casquivano(-a) scatterbrained
desconsiderado(-a) inconsiderate
frívolo(-a) frivolous
hipócrito(-a) hypocritical
ilusorio(-a) unreal, illusory

insustancial unsubstantial
necio(-a) silly
ocioso(-a) idle
poco productivo(-a) unproductive
superfluo(-a) superfluous
vanidoso(-a) vain

related terms and expressions

cantinflear to talk with double meanings, be full of hot air (like the comedian Cantinflas) [L Am]
decir lugares comunes to speak in clichés
hablar babosadas to talk nonsense [L Am]
hablar chorradas to talk nonsense [Spain]
hablar sandeces/tonterías to talk nonsense
levantar una cortina de humo to use smoke and mirrors (*lit.*, to raise a curtain of smoke)
ser una persona plástica to be a shallow or artificial person (*lit.*, a plastic person) (*colloq.*) [parts of L Am]
tener la cabeza hueca to be an airhead

cabeza *f* **de chorlito** birdbrain
cháchara *f* chitchat, superficial conversation
fachada *f* façade, appearance

Legal problems? What legal problems? Relax, man. Have a cold drink ...

¿Problemas legales? ¿Qué problemas legales? Tranquilo, hombre. Sírvete una bebida fría...

synonyms and similar words

a gusto at ease, comfortable
apacible gentle, mild
calmado(-a) calm
calmoso(-a) laid back, somewhat lazy
cul cool (*colloq.*) [Mex, parts of L Am]

ecuánime even-tempered, calm
flemático(-a) sluggish, phlegmatic
impasible impassive, not emotional
plácido(-a) placid, calm
sereno(-a) serene
tranquilo(-a) tranquil

related terms and expressions

Cálmate.	Calm down.
No es para tanto.	It's not so bad / not such a big deal.
No te comas el coco.	Don't worry. / Don't sweat it. (*lit.,* Don't eat your head.) [Spain]
No te pongas cerril.	Don't get uptight. [Spain]
No te rompes la cabeza.	Don't worry about it. / Don't sweat it.
Suave.	Take it easy. [Carib]
Tranquilízate.	Calm down.

ser más fresco(-a) que una lechuga to be cool as a cucumber (*lit.,* as a head of lettuce)
tomar las cosas con calma to take things calmly

What
a prude!

She's so stiff
and tense,
it's scary.

¡Qué mojigata!

Es tan rígida y tan tensa que causa temor.

Parece que se ha tragado un palo de escoba.

She looks
like she
swallowed a
broomstick.

synonyms and similar words

afectado(-a) affected
austero(-a) austere
delicado(-a) fussy, delicate
estirado(-a) stuffy, stuck-up
  [Spain, L Am except Mex]
estricto(-a) strict
inflexible inflexible
melindroso(-a) finicky, fastidious

mojigato(-a) sanctimonious,
  prudish, hypocritical
púdico(-a) prudish
remilgado(-a) fussy, picky
severo(-a) strict, stern
tenso(-a) tense
tieso(-a) stiff

related terms and expressions

no aguantar pulgas to be a fussbudget, be easily irritated
  (*lit.*, to not put up with fleas)
ser de los (las) mírame y no me toques to be touchy or standoffish
  (*lit.*, to be a look-at-me-but-don't-touch-me)
ser de pocas pulgas to be a fussbudget (*lit.*, to be of few fleas) [L Am]
ser más serio(-a) que burro en lancha to be uptight (*lit.*, more serious
  than a burro in a small boat) [CR]
ser un(a) tiquismiquis to be fussy or uptight
tener cara de pocos amigos to look unsociable or unfriendly
  (*lit.*, to have the face of few friends)

Your friend is very quiet, isn't she?

Tu amiga es muy callada, ¿verdad?

Sí. Su lema es "Por la boca muere el pez."

Yes. Her motto is "Loose lips sink ships" (lit., "Because of its mouth the fish dies.")

synonyms and similar words

discreto(-a) discreet
lacónico(-a) laconic, using few words
retraído(-a) withdrawn, shy

silencioso(-a) silent, quiet
taciturno(-a) taciturn, silent
tranquilo(-a) quiet

related terms and expressions

A buen entendedor, pocas palabras. (REFRÁN)
For a good listener, not many words are needed.

En boca cerrada no entran moscas. (REFRÁN)
Loose lips sink ships. (*lit.*, In the closed mouth, flies do not enter.)

Es mejor pensar que locamente hablar. (REFRÁN)
It's better to think than to spout off (*lit.*, talk crazily).

No dice "Esta boca es mía."
She doesn't say a word. (*lit.*, She doesn't say "This mouth is mine.")

No dice ni mu.
She doesn't say a word. (*lit.*, She doesn't even say moo.)

No dice ni pío.
You don't hear a peep out of her. (*lit.*, She doesn't say peep.)

Pone un zíper en la boca.
He won't say a word (*lit.*, puts a zipper on his mouth). [Mex, C Am, Ven]

Pone una cremallera en la boca.
She won't say a word (*lit.*, puts a zipper on her mouth).

He tires us out, talking so much.

What a gab session!

Nos tiene cansados de tanto hablar.

¡Qué cotorreo!

Habla hasta por los codos.

He talks a blue streak (lit., through his elbows).

Stop hogging the phone.

Deja de monopolizar el teléfono.

Bla, bla, bla...

Blah, blah, blah ...

synonyms and similar words

charlatán (charlatana) chatty (*colloq.*)
chismoso(-a) gossipy, given to gossip
comunicativo(-a) communicative
gárrulo(-a) garrulous

indiscreto(-a) indiscreet
locuaz loquacious
parlanchín (parlanchina) chatty (*colloq.*)

related terms and expressions

¡Qué cotorro(-a)! What a chatterbox!
Tiene mucha labia. She has the gift of gab (*lit.*, a lot of lip). (*can be pejorative*)
Tiene mucho rollo. He is a windbag. (*lit.*, He has a lot of roll.) (*colloq.*)
Tiene un pico de oro. He has the gift of gab (*lit.*, a golden beak).

habla que te habla blah, blah, blah

cantinflear to talk nonsense, be full of hot air (like the comedian Cantinflas) [L Am]

cotorrear to jabber away

hablar como un papagayo/perico to talk a blue streak (*lit.*, to talk like a parrot)

soltar un rollo to hold forth, rattle on

cháchara *f* chitchat
palabrería *f* hot air, wordy chatter
parrafada *f* long conversation, soliloquy

In life we have to find our own path.

En la vida hay que buscar nuestro propio sendero.

Aunt Isabel isn't afraid of anything.

Tía Isabel no le tiene miedo a nada.

Cuando crezca, quiero tener agallas como tía Isabel.

When I grow up, I want to be gutsy like Aunt Isabel.

Es muy arriesgada.

She's fearless.

synonyms and similar words

arriesgado(-a) willing to take risks, daring
atrevido(-a) daring
audaz bold, audacious
centrado(-a) centered, focused
cierto(-a) certain
dinámico(-a) dynamic
fresco(-a) sassy, fresh, a bit rude (*lit.,* fresh, cool)
impresionante impressive
intrépido(-a) intrepid, bold
seguro(-a) confident, sure
valiente valiant

related terms and expressions

hablar con aplomo to speak with confidence
ser muy vivo(-a) to be a go-getter, be sharp (*lit.,* to be very lively)
   (*often in the sense of being willing to take advantage of others*)
tener confianza en sí mismo(-a) to have self-confidence
tener mucha cara/jeta to have a lot of nerve (*lit.,* face) [Spain]
tomar la iniciativa to take the initiative

I hate to be a bother to you.

Siento molestarte.

No te preocupes por mí.

Don't mind me.

synonyms and similar words

apocado(-a) timid, dejected
aprensivo(-a) apprehensive
avergonzado(-a) embarrassed
cohibido(-a) inhibited
humilde humble
incómodo(-a) awkward, ill at ease
indeciso(-a) indecisive
miedoso(-a) fearful
retraído(-a) withdrawn, shy
ruborizado(-a) blushing
temeroso(-a) frightened
tímido(-a) bashful, shy
vacilante hesitant

related terms and expressions

carecer de autoestima to lack self-esteem
carecer de confianza en sí mismo(-a) to lack self-confidence
estar acomplejado(-a) por to have a complex about
ponerse como un tomate to turn red as a beet (*lit.*, as a tomato)
ser el último mono to be the low man on the totem pole (*lit.*, to be the last monkey) [Spain]

I love to be with people.

I'm a friendly person; what can I say?

Everyone likes him.

He's the sweetest man!

This is the way people should live.

synonyms and similar words

abierto(-a) open
afable affable
agradable agreeable
amable nice, kind
amigable friendly
amoroso(-a) loving

cálido(-a) warm
cariñoso(-a) affectionate
comunicativo(-a) communicative
extrovertido(-a) extroverted
gregario(-a) gregarious
simpático(-a) nice, likeable

related terms and expressions

Somos amigos del alma. We're best buddies / soul mates.
(*lit.*, We're friends of the soul.)

Tu amigo me cae bien. I like your friend. (*lit.*, Your friend strikes me positively.)

comer en el mismo plato to be close friends (*lit.*, to eat on the same plate)
estar enchufado(-a) to be in the loop (*lit.*, to be plugged in)
llevarse bien con to get along well with
ser uña y carne to be close friends / bosom buddies (*lit.*, to be fingernail and flesh)
tener buenas conexiones to have good connections
tener don de gente to be a people person, get on well with people (*lit.*, to have a gift for people)
tener un conecte to have a connection [Mex, parts of C Am]
tener un enchufe to have a connection [Carib, Spain]

synonyms and similar words

apartado(-a) marginalized
arisco(-a) standoffish, unfriendly
distante distant, detached
encerrado(-a) en sí mismo(-a)
  withdrawn (*lit.*, closed up in oneself)
frío(-a) cold
huraño(-a) sullen, unsociable
insociable unsociable

intratable unsociable, hard to
  deal with
introvertido(-a) introverted
misántropo(-a) misanthropic
reservado(-a) reserved
retraído(-a) withdrawn, shy
solano(-a) all on one's own
  (*from* **solo(-a)**) (*colloq.*) [L Am]

related terms and expressions

estar sin padre ni madre ni perro que me ladre to be all alone
  (*lit.*, to be without a father or mother or a dog who barks for me)
guardar las distancias to keep one's distance
no casarse con nadie to stay independent, keep one's own opinions and
  not take sides
no tener arte ni parte to have no part in

ermitaño(-a) *m/f* hermit
inadaptable *m/f* social misfit; *adj* antisocial
inconformista *m/f* nonconformist; *adj* nonconformist
individualista *m/f* individualist; *adj* individualistic
lobo *m* **solitario** lone wolf
paria *m* outcast

Let's see: bread, cheese, sodas, kids, husband ...

A ver: pan, queso, refrescos, niños, esposo...

Todo está listo ya.

Everything is ready.

synonyms and similar words

listo(-a) ready
meticuloso(-a) meticulous
metódico(-a) methodical

ordenado(-a) orderly, tidy
sistemático(-a) systematic

related terms and expressions

Hombre prevenido vale por dos. (REFRÁN)
The man who is prepared is worth two men.

Más vale prevenir que lamentar. (REFRÁN)
It's better to be prepared than to have regrets later.

acomodar to put away, put in its place
administrar to administer
arreglar to arrange
dirigir to direct (*for example,* a business, a symphony)
estar en su lugar to be in its place
estar previsto(-a) to be planned/foreseen
manejar to manage (*for example,* money, a house)
no dejar nada al azar to not leave anything to chance
pensar en todo to think of everything
pensar hacer algo to plan to do something
planificarlo todo to plan everything
preparar to prepare
tener un plan to have a plan

My disorgani-zation? What disorganiza-tion? I know exactly where I keep my things.

¿Mi desorganización? ¿Qué desorganización? Yo sé exactamente dónde mantengo mis cosas.

Lo que necesito está en medio de todo este papeleo.

What I need is somewhere in all this paperwork.

synonyms and similar words

alborotado(-a) messy, disheveled
caótico(-a) chaotic
desordenado(-a) untidy, messy
embrollado(-a) confused, mixed up

enredado(-a) tangled, knotted
extraviado(-a) misplaced
mezclado(-a) mixed up
revuelto(-a) mixed up, in a mess

related terms and expressions

estar en completo desorden to be in complete disorder
estar hecho(-a) un desastre to be in shambles (*lit.*, to be made a disaster)
estar manga por hombro to be topsy-turvy (*lit.*, to be sleeve for shoulder)
hacer algo al tuntún to do something haphazardly [S Cone, Spain]
no tener pies ni cabeza to have no order or logic (*lit.*, feet or head)
poner todo patas arriba to turn everything upside down
ser una auténtica cochambre to be a real dump

a diestra y siniestra all over the place (*lit.*, to right and left)
a troche y moche willy-nilly, pell-mell
patas arriba topsy-turvy
sin ton ni son without rhyme or reason (*lit.*, without tone or sound)

barullo *m* mess, uproar
◐ **desmadre** *m* mess [Mex, C Am, Spain]
◐ **despelote** *m* mess
embrollo *m* mess, fix
◐ **follón** *m* damn mess [Spain]

jaleo *m* mess, uproar
lío *m* mess, clutter
menjurje *m* mess [Mex, Spain]
reguero *m* mess [Carib]

workaholic | trabajólico(-a)

I don't have time to fool around.

No tengo tiempo para tonterías.

Tengo un montón de cosas que hacer.

I've got a zillion (lit., heap of) things to do.

I'm up to here (lit., to the crown of my head) with work.

Estoy hasta la coronilla de trabajo.

¡No pienso parar hasta que termine!

I'm not planning to stop until I'm finished!

synonyms and similar words

activo(-a) active
asiduo(-a) hardworking, assiduous
concienzudo(-a) conscientious
diligente diligent
hacendoso(-a) hardworking
  (*especially in context of housework*)

incansable tireless
industrioso(-a) industrious
ocupado(-a) busy
productivo(-a) productive
trabajador(a) hardworking

related terms and expressions

¡Dale duro!	Give it all you've got!
Ella no descansa ni un minuto.	She doesn't rest a minute.
Es trabajadora como una hormiga.	She's busy as a bee (*lit.*, as hardworking as an ant).
Se mata trabajando.	He kills himself working.
Trabaja a brazo partido.	She works to the max (*lit.*, to a broken arm).
Trabaja como un burro.	He works like a dog (*lit.*, like a burro).
Trabaja día y noche.	She works day and night.

chupatintas *m/f* drudge, paper pusher (*lit.*, ink sucker)
cumplidor(-a) *m/f* someone who always does what he or she promises;
  adj reliable
empollón (empollona) *m/f* someone who works or studies hard; grind,
  drudge (*colloq.*) [Spain, parts of L Am]

36 *character and personality*

If you have an urge to work ...

Si tienes ganas de trabajar,...

... siéntate, que ya se te pasará.

... sit down and it will go away.

synonyms and similar words

aplatanado(-a) lazy, lying around like a couch potato [Mex, Carib, Spain]
atenido(-a) lazy, letting others do things [Mex, C Am]
desocupado(-a) idle
flojo(-a) lazy [Mex, C Am, Carib, Chile]

haragán (haragana) lazy
holgazán (holgazana) lazy
inactivo(-a) inactive
indolente indolent, lazy
ocioso(-a) idle
torpe slow, lazy

related terms and expressions

Camina como si tuviera plomo en los zapatos.
He walks as if he had lead in his shoes.

Camina tan despacio la pereza que pronto la alcanza la pobreza. (REFRÁN)
Laziness walks so slowly that soon poverty catches up with it.

No se mata en el trabajo.
He doesn't kill himself working.

No sirve para nada.
She's good for nothing.

Que lo haga Rita.
Let someone else (*lit.*, Rita) do it.

Se hace el remolón.
He just lazes around.

Se le pegaron las sábanas.
She overslept. (*lit.*, The sheets stuck to her.)

Se mantiene con los brazos cruzados.
He twiddles his thumbs (*lit.*, keeps his arms crossed).

◗ **huevón (huevona)** *m/f* damn lazy bum [Mex, C Am, Carib]

pasota *m/f* slacker [Spain]
vago(-a) *m/f* slacker, drifter [L Am]

What type of person are you? For each of the following situations, choose the response that would most likely be yours: (a) or (b). Depending on your response, you earn one or two points. If you need help, follow the cross-reference to the page(s) indicated. Answer the questions and add up your score.

1 • You have to make a decision quickly. ☞ 2–3
   a Agarras el toro por las astas. (1)
   b Titubeas y estás entre dos aguas. (2)

2 • Two friends are giving you some new information about a political issue, something that goes against a prejudice you hold. ☞ 2–3
   a Cambias de opinión fácilmente. (1)
   b Te mantienes en tus trece a pesar de todo. (2)

3 • Your sister needs to borrow some money. ☞ 10–11
   a No le das ni la hora. (2)
   b Das hasta la camisa para ayudarla. (1)

4 • One of your friends has a problem with his computer and needs your help. ☞ 12–13
   a Te importa un pepino. (2)
   b Lo sacas de un apuro. (1)

5 • A friend asks you to intervene in a delicate situation. ☞ 12–13
   a Le echas una mano y sacas la cara por él. (1)
   b Le dices que no te interesa en lo más mínimo. (2)

6 • You get a big pay raise. ☞ 16–17
   a Empiezas a fanfarronear. (2)
   b No le dices nada a nadie para no llamar la atención. (1)

7 • Your brother calls you and asks you to help him solve a big problem
     that he brought on himself. ☞ 18–19
   a Le dices que puede contar contigo. (1)
   b Le das mucha lata. (2)

8 • You're describing your general outlook on the world. ☞ 20–21
   a Lo ves todo negro y siempre temes lo peor. (2)
   b Crees en tu estrella y siempre ves el lado positivo de las cosas. (1)

9 • The driver in the lane next to you insults you. ☞ 22–23
   a Le contestas con buena educación. (1)
   b Le contestas con una palabrota. (2)

10 • Your cousin needs your input on an important decision. ☞ 24–25
   a Vas al fondo de las cosas. (1)
   b Levantas una cortina de humo y le contestas con lugares comunes. (2)

11 • It's time to do your taxes, but you can't find all your receipts. ☞ 26–27
   a Te pones tan tenso(-a) que causa temor. (2)
   b Eres más fresco(-a) que una lechuga. (1)

12 • Your roommate needs to use the phone. ☞ 28–29
   a Sigues hablando hasta por los codos. (2)
   b Dejas de monopolizar el teléfono. (1)

13 • You're describing how you usually behave at a social event where you
     don't know many people. ☞ 28–29
   a No dices ni mu. (1)
   b Tienes un pico de oro. (2)

14 • You get to meet your favorite movie star. ☞ 30–31
   a Te pones tímido(-a) y avergonzado(-a). (2)
   b Tomas la iniciativa para hablarle; te sientes seguro(-a) de ti
     mismo(-a). (1)

15 • You're at a neighborhood block party. ☞ 32–33
   a Te llevas bien con todo el mundo. (2)
   b Guardas las distancias porque la gente te incomoda. (1)

16 • It's your turn to plan the company picnic. ☞ 34–35
   a Haces las cosas a troche y moche. (2)
   b Piensas en todo y no dejas nada al azar. (1)

17 • Important visitors have come to your company. Your boss wants to bring
     them around to see you, and they find you in your office. ☞ 34–35
   a Es una auténtica cochambre. (2)
   b Todo está en su lugar. (1)

18 • In general, you have a certain approach whenever you clean the house or mow the lawn. ☞ 36–37
   a Trabajas como un burro. (1)
   b Caminas como si tuvieras plomo en los zapatos. (2)

19 • Someone wakes you up in the middle of the night. ☞ 42
   a Reaccionas de manera brusca y malhumorada. (2)
   b Lo perdonas y vuelves a dormir. (1)

20 • People you work with describe you. ☞ 42
   a Es una persona muy equilibrada; nunca se enoja. (1)
   b No es perita en dulce. (2)

21 • There's a scandal in your office. ☞ 50
   a Corres inmediatamente a tu jefe con los chismes. (2)
   b No dices ni mu de la situación, calladito(-a) como una tumba. (1)

22 • You're at a party. ☞ 58
   a Eres el corazón del grupo. (1)
   b Pones a todos a dormir con una larga anécdota. (2)

23 • There's a problem in the kitchen just before your dinner guests arrive. ☞ 60
   a Tratas de solucionarlo calmadamente. (1)
   b Te sales de las casillas. (2)

24 • At work, someone criticizes you and wants to do things his way. ☞ 62
   a Tratas de hacer un compromiso y hacer las paces. (1)
   b Te enojas y sales de la oficina. (2)

25 • You have to open the office very early tomorrow morning. ☞ 65
   a Se puede confiar en ti. (1)
   b Seguro que no cumplirás con este deber. (2)

To see how you did on the personality test, turn to page 72.

How affectionate he is!

Yes, he's very friendly.

¡Qué cariñoso!

Sí, es muy amigable.

Nos quiere a todos.

He loves us all.

synonyms and similar words

amoroso(-a) loving
cálido(-a) warm, friendly
dulce sweet

meloso(-a) sweet as honey
mimoso(-a) cuddly, affectionate
tierno(-a) tender

related terms and expressions

Está tan mimado(-a) que está echado(-a) a perder.   He's/She's so spoiled he's/she's ruined.

acariciar to caress; to pet
besar con la lengua to French kiss (*lit.,* to kiss with the tongue)
besuquearse to smooch, kiss repeatedly; to make out
chiquear to spoil, treat like a child [Mex, Cuba]
consentir to spoil
contemplar demasiado to spoil, coddle (*lit.,* to admire too much)
mimar to spoil

abrazo *m* hug
abrazote *m* big hug
beso *m* kiss
besote *m* big kiss
caricia *f* caress, cuddle
cariño *m* affection; darling
corazón *m* darling (*lit.,* heart)
dulzura *f* sweetie

luz *f* **de mi vida** light of my life
m'hijo(-a) *m/f* my dear
   (*lit.,* my son/daughter)
mi cielo *m* my love, dear (*lit.,* my heaven)
mi tesoro *m* my love, dear
   (*lit.,* my treasure)
mi vida *f* my love, dear (*lit.,* my life)

Am I getting this glass of water today or tomorrow?

Y ¿tendré que esperar hasta mañana para que me traigan un vaso de agua?

¡Increíble! Me puedo morir de sed en este momento y a nadie le importa.

Incredible! I could die of thirst now and no one cares.

¡Ésta es una familia de desconsiderados!

This family is a bunch of inconsiderates!

synonyms and similar words

áspero(-a) rough, surly
belicoso(-a) bellicose
brusco(-a) gruff, brusque
combativo(-a) contentious
de mal genio bad-tempered
desapacible nasty, disagreeable

malhumorado(-a) crabby
peleador(a) prone to fighting
pendenciero(-a) quarrelsome
provocador(a) provocative
tosco(-a) rough, uncouth
violento(-a) violent

related terms and expressions

Le gusta discutir/pelear/reñir. He likes to argue/fight/quarrel.
Lo dejó hecho polvo/puré. She made mincemeat out of him.
No es perita en dulce. She's a tough cookie. (*lit.*, She's no pear in sugar water.)

No se puede con ella. She's impossible. (*lit.*, You can't with her.)
Nos comerá vivos. He'll eat us alive.
Nos regaña a todos. She tells us all off.
Siempre lleva la contraria. He always contradicts people (*lit.*, takes the opposite side).

Tiene muy mala leche. She's a grump (*lit.*, has very bad milk).

buscapleitos *m/f* troublemaker
enojón (enojona) *m/f* hothead
fosforito *m/f* hothead (*lit.*, little match) [parts of L Am]
gruñón (gruñona) *m/f* grouch, grumbler

And then, blah, blah, blah ...

Y después, bla, bla, bla...

Nos aburrimos como una ostra.

Es capaz de dormir a un muerto.

Parece que no tiene fin.

¡Qué lata!

¡Qué aburrido!

We were bored stiff (lit., bored as an oyster).

She could put a dead person to sleep.

There's just no end to it.

What a drag!

How boring!

synonyms and similar words

desagradable disagreeable
fastidioso(-a) annoying, tiresome
fatal deadly, horrible
laborioso(-a) laborious
latoso(-a) boring, tiresome, a pain [most of L Am]

molesto(-a) annoying
monótono(-a) monotonous
mortal deadly
pesado(-a) dull, boring
soporífico(-a) sleep-inducing
tedioso(-a) tedious

related terms and expressions

Es muy pegajoso(-a). — He's/She's a pest (*lit.*, sticky).
Es una ladilla. — He's a real pain (*lit.*, leech).
Es una lapa. — She's a pest (*lit.*, barnacle).
Es una lata. — It's a drag (*lit.*, tin can).
Estoy harto(-a) de esto. — I'm sick and tired of this.
Me tiene aburrido(-a)/hastiado(-a). — I'm fed up / bored with it.
Nos pone a todos a dormir. — It puts us all to sleep.
¡Qué cansón! — How tiresome! / What a drag!
¡Qué cruz! — What a drag (*lit.*, cross)!
Teníamos que pellizcarnos para mantenernos despiertos. — We had to pinch ourselves to stay awake.

sin chiste dull, boring (*lit.*, without joke) [Mex, C Am, S Am]
sin gracia dull, boring (*lit.*, without grace)
sin sabor insipid, flavorless (*lit.*, without taste)

I break everything I touch.

How clumsy I am!

Todo lo que toco lo rompo.

¡Qué torpe soy!

Pues, a veces eres un poco inepto.

Well, you're a little inept sometimes.

synonyms and similar words

incapaz incapable
incompetente incompetent
inexperto(-a) inexperienced

inhábil unskillful
lerdo(-a) slow, lumbering, doltish
patoso(-a) clumsy, klutzy

adoquín *m/f* oaf (*lit.*, paving stone)
zoquete *m/f* blockhead; *adj* stupid

related terms and expressions

Cometí una burrada. I made a big mistake (*lit.*, committed a drove of donkeys).

En todo meto la pata. I mess everything up (*lit.*, stick my foot into everything).

La cagué. I screwed up (*lit.*, shit it).

Todo lo estropeo. I goof everything up.

ser chambón (chambona) to do shoddy work, be someone who does a job in a clumsy way

ser un manazas to be all thumbs, be a klutz [Spain]

ser un zafio to be a klutz [Spain]

opposites

capaz capable
diestro(-a) dextrous, skillful

hábil handy
perfeccionista perfectionist

She thinks she's smarter than everybody else.

Se cree más inteligente que los demás.

Con que tratando de estafar a una estafadora, ¿eh?

Se pasó de lista.

Trying to con a con artist, eh?

She was too clever for her own good.

synonyms and similar words

abusado(-a) wily, clever [Mex]
astuto(-a) astute
avispado(-a) sharp
disimulador(a) secretive, covering up one's true intentions
engañoso(-a) deceitful

espabilado(-a) alert, bright
ingenioso(-a) ingenious
manipulador(a) manipulative
solapado(-a) sneaky
tramposo(-a) tricky, deceitful

embustero(-a) *m/f* crook, fraud, con
estafador(a) *m/f* con artist, crook
majadero(-a) *m/f* crook, con [Spain]
pícaro(-a) *m/f* rascal

telemanejes *mpl* schemes, monkey business
tracalero(-a) *m/f* crook, con artist [Mex]

related terms and expressions

Hecha la ley, hecha la trampa. (REFRÁN)   When the law is made, the scheme is laid.

disimular to hide one's true thoughts or intentions
engañar a alguien to pull the wool over someone's eyes
hacer algo a escondidas to do something on the sly
hacer algo por debajo de cuerda to do something dishonestly (*lit.,* under rope)
hacerse el vivo (la viva) to be clever at taking advantage of someone
ser tan listo como un zorro (tan lista como una zorra) to be sly as a fox

She's bonkers, isn't she?

I think this patient has slipped a gear (lit., her head is skating). [L Am]

synonyms and similar words

alocado(-a) crazy
anormal abnormal
demente demented
deschavetado(-a) nuts
  (*lit.*, headless)

desequilibrado(-a) unbalanced
lunático(-a) nuts, lunatic
trastornado(-a) deranged, disturbed
zafado(-a) nuts, berserk
  [Mex, C Am, Col, Chile]

related terms and expressions

Es un disparate.	It's crazy.
Es una locura.	It's crazy.
Está tocada de la cabeza.	She's touched in the head.
Ha perdido la razón.	He's lost his mind.
Le falla la azotea.	She has bats in her belfry. (*lit.*, Her roof is failing.)
Le falta un tornillo.	He has a screw loose (*lit.*, missing).
Se le fundieron los fusibles.	She has lost her marbles (*lit.*, has melted fuses).
Se vuelve loca.	She's going crazy.
Tiene los cables cruzados.	He's wacky. (*lit.*, He has his cables crossed.)

opposites

cuerdo(-a) sane, of sound mind
racional rational

sensato(-a) sensible

Tell your boyfriend I'm watching him.

I'm on my guard.

There's something going on!

I smell a rat. (lit., This smells bad.)

I suspect something.

I sleep with one eye open and the other closed.

You see evil everywhere!

You don't trust anybody.

I have a hunch ...

synonyms and similar words

cauteloso(-a) cautious
escéptico(-a) skeptical
paranoico(-a) paranoid
preocupado(-a) worried
receloso(-a) distrustful, having misgivings
suspicaz suspicious, mistrustful

related terms and expressions

Hay algo en él (ella) que me hace desconfiar. — Something about him/her makes me suspicious (*lit.*, not trust him/her).

Hay gato encerrado. (REFRÁN) — There's something fishy. (*lit.*, There's a cat closed up.)

Tuve un presentimiento. — I had a premonition.

opposites

confiado(-a) trusting
despreocupado(-a) unconcerned, not worrying
incauto(-a) unwary, gullible
ingenuo(-a) innocent, ingenuous

dogmatic | dogmático(-a)

No argument!

Period!

It's obvious.

It's clear as a bell. (lit., A rooster doesn't crow any clearer.)

I won't give in. (lit., I won't give my arm to twist.)

I'm 100 percent in favor!

I'm positive!

I'll fight to the death!

synonyms and similar words

autoritario(-a) authoritarian
determinado(-a) determined
dominador(a) dominating
firme firm
franco(-a) frank
imperioso(-a) imperious
implacable implacable, relentless

inflexible inflexible
inquebrantable unshakable
intransigente uncompromising
mandón (mandona) bossy
obstinado(-a) obstinate
terco(-a) stubborn

related terms and expressions

Cuando tiene una idea entre ceja y ceja, no nos deja en paz.

When she gets an idea fixed in her head (*lit.*, between eyebrow and eyebrow), she doesn't leave us in peace.

Defiende su opinión a capa y espada.

He defends his opinion to the hilt (*lit.*, with cape and sword).

absoluto(-a) absolute
claro(-a) clear
indiscutible indisputable, unquestionable
irrefutable irrefutable

It's time to give Pulpita her bottle.

Es hora de darle el biberón a Pulpita.

Es todo un personaje.

Este tipo está chiflado.

Es un bicho raro.

He's a real character.

This guy's wacko.

He's an oddball.

synonyms and similar words

bohemio(-a) bohemian
especial odd, special
estrafalario(-a) weird, outlandish
extraño(-a) strange
extravagante outlandish
inconformista nonconformist

insólito(-a) strange
original original
raro(-a) strange, odd
singular extraordinary, peculiar
único(-a) unique

related terms and expressions

Se burlan de mis rarezas. They make fun of my peculiarities.
(*referring to odd mannerisms or habits*)

excentricidad *f* eccentricity
inconformismo *m* nonconformity
manía *f* obsession, craze, mania
originalidad *f* originality
rareza *f* rarity; peculiarity
singularidad *f* uniqueness

opposites

banal banal
común y corriente common and ordinary, average

conformista conformist
normal ordinary
razonable reasonable

¡Qué lengua larga! Siempre con las antenas puestas.

What a gossip (lit., long tongue)! Always with his antennas up!

Hay que demandarlo por calumniador.

We should sue him for slander.

Ten cuidado, que es un verdadero chismoso.

Be careful; he's a real gossip.

synonyms and similar words

bocazas *m/f* blabbermouth [Spain]
bocón (bocona) *m/f* blabbermouth [L Am]
malas lenguas *fpl* malicious gossipers, rumormongers (*lit.,* bad tongues)

related terms and expressions

calumniar to slander
chismear to gossip
cotillear to gossip, jabber
curiosear to snoop (around)

denigrar to denigrate
desacreditar to discredit
difamar to slander

chisme *m* piece of gossip
chismografía *f* "gossipography," gossip or practice of spreading gossip
 (*colloq.*) (*from* **chisme** + **grafía**)
chismorreos *mpl* gossip, rumors
cotorreo *m* gossip or gab session
rumor *m* rumor

opposites

no decir ni mu to not say a word
ser callado(-a) (como una tumba) to be quiet (as a tomb)
ser discreto(-a) to be discreet

Look, everything is in order, done to perfection.

Miren, todo está en orden, hecho a la perfección.

Puedes confiar en él; es un hombre honesto.

Casi cuesta creerse.

Se le ve que es un hombre honrado, sincero, responsable y digno de confianza.

You can trust him; he's an honest man.

Almost too good to be true. (lit., It almost costs to believe.)

You can see that he's a man who is honorable, sincere, responsible, and trustworthy.

synonyms and similar words

concienzudo(-a) conscientious
confiable trustworthy
decente decent
escrupuloso(-a) scrupulous
ético(-a) ethical
honrado(-a) honest, honorable

íntegro(-a) upright
irreprochable irreproachable, blameless
leal loyal
recto(-a) upright

related terms and expressions

Al pan, pan y al vino, vino. (REFRÁN)

No te defraudará.

Su conducta es intachable.

Tell it like it is. (*lit.,* Call bread "bread" and call wine "wine.")

He won't let you down (*lit.,* defraud or cheat you).

Her behavior is impeccable.

decencia *f* decency
franqueza *f* frankness
honestidad *f* honesty

integridad *f* integrity
lealtad *f* loyalty
moral *f* morals; morale

opposites

deshonesto(-a) dishonest
desleal disloyal
mentiroso(-a) lying

sin escrúpulos with no scruples or qualms
traicionero(-a) treacherous
tramposo(-a) deceitful, tricky

I can't figure this guy out.

No puedo entender a este tipo.

Creo que oculta algo.

I think he's hiding something.

He seems two-faced.

Parece que tiene dos caras.

synonyms and similar words

disimulador(a) secretive, covering up (something)
engañoso(-a) deceitful
falso(-a) phony
manipulador(a) manipulative

mentiroso(-a) lying; *m/f* liar
mojigato(-a) sanctimonious, hypocritical
solapado(-a) sneaky
tramposo(-a) tricky, deceitful

related terms and expressions

Farol de la calle y oscuridad de su casa. (REFRÁN)
A light in the street but darkness at home.

Palabras de santo, uñas de gato. (REFRÁN)
A saint's words, but a cat's claws.

actuar con disimulo to cover up one's true thoughts or intentions
engañar a alguien to deceive someone, pull the wool over someone's eyes
hacer algo a escondidas to do something on the sly
hacer algo por debajo de la mesa to do something under the table
tener dos caras to be two-faced

diablo *m* **vendiendo cruces** hypocrite (*lit.*, the devil selling crosses)
farsante *m/f* fake, impostor
mosquita *f* **muerta** hypocrite, someone who pretends to be innocent but takes advantage of others (*lit.*, a dead fly)
santurrón (santurrona) *m/f* holier-than-thou person, goody-goody

Holy cow!
(lit., *What
barbarity!*)

You're
not at all
presentable!

How
embarrassing.
(lit., *You give
shame.*)

How can
you think
of taking the
boy like this?

¡Qué barbaridad!

¡No estás
nada
presentable!

Das
vergüenza.

¿Cómo se
te ocurre
recibir al
niño así?

Déjame
en paz.
No jodas.

Debes
traerlo
a una
hora
prudente.

Papá, ¡tu nuevo
"look" es lo máximo!

Leave me
alone.
Don't screw
with me.

You should
bring him
at a decent
hour.

Dad,
your new
look rules!

synonyms and similar words

desvergonzado(-a) shameless
escandaloso(-a) shocking,
  scandalous
grosero(-a) crude, rude
inapropiado(-a) inappropriate
incorrecto(-a) improper

inmoral immoral
obsceno(-a) obscene
plebe low-class
repugnante repugnant, disgusting
vergonzoso(-a) shameful
vil vile, despicable

related terms and expressions

¡Qué escándalo! How shocking! (*lit.,* What a scandal!)
¡Qué falta de decencia! What a lack of decency!
¡Qué modales más pésimos! What terrible manners!
¡Qué vulgar! What vulgarity! / How vulgar!

de mal gusto in bad taste

bruto(-a) *m/f* lout, brute
cerdo(-a) *m/f* pig
descarado(-a) *m/f* jerk (*lit.,* faceless one)
lépero(-a) *m/f* coarse or rude person [Mex, C Am]
naco(-a) *m/f* jerk, rude person [Mex]
patán *m* lout, lowlife
sinvergüenza *m/f* jerk (*lit.,* shameless person)

I'm a dull person. I lack spirit and liveliness.

Soy una persona muy sosa. Me falta gracia y viveza.

Pase mejor a la siguiente página.

Better just turn the page.

synonyms and similar words

banal banal
común common
corriente common, ordinary
desabrido(-a) bland, blah
desanimado(-a) dispirited, dejected
insípido(-a) insipid

insulso(-a) dull, insipid
mediocre mediocre
ordinario(-a) common, tacky
sencillo(-a) plain
soso(-a) dull, bland, boring

related terms and expressions

no ser nada del otro mundo to be nothing to write home about (*lit.,* to be nothing from the other world)
no tener chiste to be blah, dull; to be senseless or useless [L Am, not S Cone]
ser del montón to be a dime a dozen (*lit.,* of the heap)
ser el último mono to be the low man on the totem pole (*lit.,* to be the last monkey) [Spain]
ser plato de segunda mesa to be a second-class citizen, play second fiddle (*lit.,* to be a dish of the second table)
ser un don Nadie to be a nobody, be someone of no consequence

ni fu ni fa so-so, no great shakes
ni muy muy ni tan tan so-so, blah, mediocre [L Am]
gris drab, gray
sin gracia boring (*lit.,* without charm)
sin sabor flavorless, blah (*lit.,* without taste)

Allow me to introduce myself: My name is Pablo Hernández.

Déjeme presentarme: me llamo Pablo Hernández.

Señores, los dejo para que hablen entre sí.

Mucho gusto. Soy Alejandro Gutiérrez.

Gentlemen, I'll leave you so you can talk together.

My pleasure. I'm Alejandro Gutiérrez.

synonyms and similar words

conexión *f* connection
contacto *m* contact, connection
enlace *m* link
enlace *m* **sindical** union rep

intercesor(a) *m/f* intercessor
negociador(a) *m/f* negotiator
tercero *m* third party

related terms and expressions

agrupar to group
conectar dos personas to connect two people
enganchar a una persona con otra to hook one person up with another [Mex, C Am]
estar bien conectado(-a) con alguien to be well connected with someone
estar enchufado(-a) to be in the loop (*lit.,* to be plugged in)
juntar dos personas to bring two people together
mantenerse en contacto to keep in touch
poner a alguien en contacto (con) to put someone in touch (with)
presentar to introduce
reunir to bring together
servir de vínculo (entre) to serve as a link (between)
tener buenas conexiones to have good connections
tener un conecte to have a connection [Mex, parts of C Am]
tener un enchufe to have a connection [Carib, Spain]

These little darlings need to play.

Let them play— they don't bother me in the least.

Estos angelitos necesitan jugar.

Que juegen, pues ellos no me molestan en lo más mínimo.

Usted es muy amable.

Siempre tan bondadosa con todo el mundo.

You're very nice.

Always so kind to everyone.

synonyms and similar words

afectuoso(-a) loving, affectionate
amable amiable, friendly
amistoso(-a) friendly
amoroso(-a) loving
apacible gentle, mild
cálido(-a) warm
cariñoso(-a) affectionate
comprensivo(-a) understanding
cordial cordial
dulce sweet

ecuánime even-tempered
indulgente indulgent
llevadero(-a) easy to get along with, bearable
paciente patient
pacífico(-a) peaceful
sereno(-a) serene
simpático(-a) nice
tolerante tolerant

related terms and expressions

Eres más bueno(-a) que el pan.	You're as good as gold. (*lit.*, You're better than bread.)
Eres muy buena gente.	You're a great person.
Eres un amor.	You're a dear (*lit.*, a love).
Eres una joya.	You're a gem.
Tienes buen corazón.	You have a good heart.
Tienes un corazón de oro.	You have a heart of gold.

He's very
dynamic;
he knows
how to
motivate
people.

He's a
natural-born
leader.

Reúne y organiza a la gente por el bien común de todos.

Es muy dinámico; sabe motivar a la gente.

Tiene mucha carisma, ¿no?

Es un líder natural.

He unites
and
organizes
people for
the common
good.

He has
a lot of
charisma,
doesn't he?

synonyms and similar words

amos *mpl* **del cotarro** the ones in charge (*lit.*, masters of the bank of the ravine) [Spain]

caudillo *m* leader (*usually military*)

cerebro *m* the brains

dirigente *m/f* leader (of a party or union), manager (of a business)

empleador(a) *m/f* employer

encargado(-a) *m/f* person in charge

entrenador(a) *m/f* coach

guía *m/f* guide

jefazos (jefazas) *mpl/fpl* honchos, bosses

jefe (jefa) *m/f* boss

maestro(-a) *m/f* master, teacher

mero mero (mera mera) *m/f* top dog [Mex, northern C Am]

patrón (patrona) *m/f* boss

pez gordo *m* big shot (*lit.*, fat fish)

responsable *m/f* person responsible

superior *m/f* superior

supervisor(a) *m/f* supervisor

related terms and expressions

llevar bien puestos los pantalones to wear the pants, be in charge (*lit.*, wear the pants well placed)

llevar la batuta to be in charge (*lit.*, carry the baton)

llevar la voz cantante to call the shots (*lit.*, carry the singing voice)

tener la sartén por el mango to have the upper hand, be in charge (*lit.*, have the skillet by the handle)

Wait, then the psychiatrist says ...

Espera, entonces el psiquiatra dice...

¡Este tipo es tan divertido!

Él sí sabe contar una historia.

¡Me muero de la risa!

Es el corazón del grupo.

¡Es una fábrica de chistes!

This guy's so entertaining!

He sure knows how to tell a story.

He's killing me!

He's the life of the party (lit., the heart of the group).

He's a joke machine!

synonyms and similar words

alma *f* **del grupo** life of the party (*lit.,* soul of the group)
bromista *m/f* joker, prankster
bufón (bufona) *m/f* jester, kidder, entertainer
comediante *m/f* comedian
fiestero(-a) *m/f* party animal

juerguista *m/f* party animal
payaso *m* clown
trasnochador(a) *m/f* night owl, someone who's out all night / up all night
vacilón (vacilona) *m/f* cut-up, comic, jokester

related terms and expressions

¿Has oído el último? Have you heard the latest (joke)?
¡La historia se complica! The plot thickens!
¡Qué chistoso! How funny!

gastar bromas to banter
hacer payasadas to clown around

vacilar to joke around, kid

cómico(-a) funny, comical
divertido(-a) amusing
entretenido(-a) entertaining
genial amusing, witty

gracioso(-a) funny
jovial jovial
ocurrente witty

anécdota *f* anecdote
broma *f* joke
chiste *m* **verde** dirty (*lit.,* green) joke

fiesta *f* **animada** lively party
historia *f* **graciosa** funny story
juego *m* **de palabras** pun

el/la perdedor(a) — loser

Everything was against me, that's for sure.

De seguro, todo estaba en mi contra.

El gobierno no me ayuda.

The government doesn't help me.

Blame it on bad luck …

Échale la culpa a la mala suerte …

Para la edad de seis años, ya nuestro destino ha sido determinado.

By age six, our future's been determined.

What a shame!

¡Qué lástima!

synonyms and similar words

amargado(-a) embittered
deplorable deplorable
humillado(-a) humiliated
inútil worthless
lamentable sad, regrettable
patético(-a) pathetic
vencido(-a) defeated

cero *m* **a la izquierda** dead loss, loser (*lit.*, zero to the left)
dejado(-a) *m/f* loser, slacker [C Am, Chile]
fracasado(-a) *m/f* failure; loser
mequetrefe *m/f* good-for-nothing, loser
perdedor(a) *m/f* loser
quedado(-a) *m/f* loser (*lit.*, left behind) [CR, northern L Am]

related terms and expressions

La despidieron.	They fired her.
La suspendieron. Suspendió.	They flunked her. She flunked.
Lo catearon.	They flunked him. [Spain]
Lo corrieron.	They fired/dumped him (*lit.*, ran him off).
Lo mandaron por un tubo.	They dumped him (*lit.*, sent him through a pipe). [Mex, C Am]
Lo tronaron. Tronó.	They flunked him. He flunked. [Mex]

caerse con todo el equipo to completely blow it, be a total washout (*lit.*, to fall with all the equipment)
no servir para nada to be good for nothing

¡Esto es sumamente grave!

¡Es un asunto de vida o muerte!

¡Es algo catastrófico!

¡Estoy muerto de miedo!

¡Es espeluznante!

This is extremely serious!

It's a matter of life and death!

It's a catastrophe!

I'm scared to death!

It's terrifying (lit., hair-raising)!

synonyms and similar words

desgarrador(a) heart-wrenching
dramático(-a) dramatic
emotivo(-a) emotional
exagerado(-a) exaggerated
excesivo(-a) excessive

extremo(-a) extreme
patético(-a) pathetic
sensible sensitive
teatral theatrical

related terms and expressions

Este tipo es demasiado.	This guy's too much.
Le gusta hacer teatro.	She likes to put on an act.
Montó un numerito.	He made a scene (*lit.*, put on a little number).
No se mide.	She's really something (*lit.*, doesn't measure herself).
Se está pasando de la raya.	He's going too far (*lit.*, passing over the line).
Se salió de las casillas.	She went overboard (*lit.*, out of her little boxes).

opposites

equilibrado(-a) balanced, even-tempered
moderado(-a) reasonable, moderate
normal normal

ponderado(-a) level-headed
sensato(-a) sensible

Let's come to an agreement.

Pongámonos de acuerdo.

Me importa lo mismo ocho que ochenta.

It's all the same to me. (lit., *Eight and eighty are of the same importance to me.*)

It's okay.

Está bien.

Yo no soy nada complicada.

I'm not all that difficult.

I don't care either way.

Me da igual.

Vive y deja vivir.

Live and let live.

synonyms and similar words

acomodadizo(-a) accommodating
benevolente benevolent
bondadoso(-a) good-natured, kind
comprensivo(-a) understanding
dócil compliant, docile
dulce sweet
ecuánime even-tempered
flexible flexible
indulgente indulgent
moderado(-a) moderate
tranquilo(-a) calm, easy-going

related terms and expressions

Es una persona muy llevadera.   She is easy to get along with.

peacemaker | el/la mediador(a)

synonyms and similar words

árbitro(-a) *m/f* referee
intermediario(-a) *m/f* intermediary
intérprete *m/f* interpreter
negociador(a) *m/f* negotiator

related terms and expressions

conciliar to reconcile
encontrar un término medio to find a middle ground
hacer las paces to make peace
hacer un compromiso to compromise
ponerse de acuerdo to come to an agreement

apacible gentle, mild
pacífico(-a) peaceful
sereno(-a) serene
sosegado(-a) calm
tranquilo(-a) tranquil, calm

opposites

agresivo(-a) aggressive
hostil hostile
violento(-a) violent

He thinks he's hot stuff (lit., the very very). And his kid is just as snotty as he is.

Yeah, they think they're God's gift.

They love to show off.

How stuck-up they are!

They're really arrogant.

synonyms and similar words

arrogante arrogant
creído(-a) stuck-up
desdeñoso(-a) disdainful
encopetado(-a) haughty, acting high-class
engreído(-a) stuck-up
esnob snobbish

estirado(-a) stuck-up
[Spain, L Am except Mex]
orgulloso(-a) proud
pedante pedantic
presumido(-a) stuck-up
presuntuoso(-a) presumptuous
soberbio(-a) proud

related terms and expressions

¡Qué esnob!	What a snob!
Se cree el (la) muy muy.	He/She thinks he's/she's hot stuff (*lit.,* the very very).
Se cree la divina garza/ pomada.	He thinks he's God's gift (*lit.,* the divine heron/ointment).
Se cree la gran cosa.	He thinks he's God's gift (*lit.,* the big thing).
Se cree la última Coca-Cola en el desierto.	He thinks he's God's gift (*lit.,* the last Coca-Cola in the desert).
Se hace el pez gordo.	He acts like a big shot. (*lit.,* He makes himself the fat fish.)
Tiene muchos humos.	He's full of himself. (*lit.,* He has a lot of smoke).

From my office I can see my cars. They remind me that my business is going great guns (lit., *with the wind at the stern*).

Desde mi oficina puedo ver mis automóviles. Al mirarlos, me acuerdo de que mis negocios van viento en popa.

synonyms and similar words

acomodado(-a) comfortable, with means
adinerado(-a) wealthy, moneyed
afortunado(-a) fortunate
forrado(-a) rich (*lit.,* with lined pockets)

opulento(-a) opulent
platudo(-a) rich (*colloq.*) [L Am]
prolífico(-a) prolific
rico(-a) rich

related terms and expressions

estar podrido(-a) de dinero to be filthy rich
ganar mucha plata to make big bucks
hacer su agosto to make hay while the sun shines, make a killing (*lit.,* make one's August)

abundante abundant
floreciente flourishing
fructífero(-a) fruitful
lucrativo(-a) lucrative
productivo(-a) productive

hijo(-a) *m/f* **de papi** rich kid (*lit.,* Daddy's son/daughter) (*colloq.*)
millonario(-a) *m/f* millionaire
millonetis *m/f* millionaire (*colloq.*) [Spain]
ricachón (ricachona) *m/f* Richy Rich, very rich person (*colloq.*)

Yes, she's a person you can trust.

Is Yolanda trustworthy?

I would give her my keys without thinking twice about it.

Sí, es una persona de confianza.

Verdaderamente inspira confianza.

Le daré mis llaves sin pensarlo dos veces.

¿Se puede confiar en Yolanda?

Es muy responsable.

Puedes contar con ella.

Siempre cumple con sus deberes.

She really inspires confidence.

She's very responsible.

You can count on her.

She always keeps her obligations (lit., fulfills her duties).

synonyms and similar words

concienzudo(-a) conscientious
escrupuloso(-a) scrupulous
formal serious-minded, dependable
honrado(-a) honest, upright
meticuloso(-a) meticulous

puntual punctual
responsable responsible
serio(-a) serious
trabajador(a) hardworking

related terms and expressions

Ella nunca te defraudará. She'll never let you down.
Es de confianza. He's trustworthy.
Es muy cumplido(-a). He's/She's reliable.
Es muy cumplidor(a). He's/She's reliable.
Se puede confiar en él (ella). You can trust him/her.

opposites

informal undependable, not likely to follow the norms of behavior
irresponsable irresponsible
negligente negligent
perezoso(-a) lazy

cantamañanas *m/f* flake [Spain]
faltón (faltona) *m/f* person who doesn't come through or keep his/her word
tardón (tardona) *m/f* slow or late person

I respect your right to enjoy your free time, but ...

Respeto tu derecho a disfrutar de tus ratos libres, pero...

¿Qué? ¿Te molestan mis puercoespines?

Bien sabes cuánto te adoran.

What? Do my porcupines annoy you?

You know how they adore you.

synonyms and similar words

atento(-a) attentive
considerado(-a) considerate
cortés polite

atención *f* attention
consideración *f* consideration
cortesía *f* courtesy

deferente deferential
solícito(-a) solicitous

cuidado *m* care
deferencia *f* deference
respeto *m* respect

related terms and expressions

No me faltes el respeto.   Don't talk back. / Don't disrespect me.
  (said to children)

hablar con tacto to speak tactfully
llevar a alguien en palmitas to treat someone like a king or queen
   (*lit.*, to carry with palm leaves)
tener entre algodones a alguien to handle someone with kid gloves
   (*lit.*, to have someone between cottons)
tratar como un rey (una reina) to treat like a king/queen

opposites

desatención *f* lack of respect/consideration
desprecio *m* contempt
falta *f* **de respeto** lack of respect

He loves me, he loves me not ...

It's not love; it's passion.

This guy makes me weak in the knees.

Stop putting me on (lit., saying nonsense); what you want is a fling.

Me ama, no me ama...

¡Qué apasionado!

No es amor; es pasión.

Te amo. Te adoro. Te amaré por el resto de mi vida.

¡Estoy loco por ti!

Este tipo me hace temblar hasta las rodillas.

Para de decir tonterías; lo que quieres es una aventura amorosa.

No dejo de pensar en ti ni de día ni de noche.

What ardor!

I love you. I adore you. I'll love you for the rest of my life.

I'm crazy about you!

I can't stop thinking about you day or night.

related terms and expressions

Nadie es perfecto hasta que te enamoras de él (ella). (REFRÁN)
No one's perfect until you fall in love with him/her.

Te amo hoy más que ayer y menos que mañana.
I love you today more than yesterday and less than tomorrow.

adorar a alguien to adore someone
andar de novios to be sweethearts
echar flores to compliment, praise (*lit.*, to throw flowers)
echar piropos to give street compliments
enamorarse to fall in love
encariñarse con alguien to get attached to someone, feel affection for someone
estar comprometido(-a) con alguien, a punto de casarse to be committed/ engaged to someone, on the verge of marriage
estar locamente enamorado(-a) to be madly in love
estar perdidamente enamorado(-a) to be madly in love
quedar flechado(-a) to be smitten, fall in love at first sight (*lit.*, to be left struck by an arrow (Cupid's))
ser un caballero to be a gentleman
tener el corazón en la mano to wear one's heart on one's sleeve
tener el corazón roto to be heartbroken

piropos *mpl* street compliments

He's famous. His name's on the front page of the newspaper.

Es famoso. Su nombre sale en la primera página del periódico.

¡Este tipo es lo máximo! ¡Es estupendo!

This guy rocks! He's great!

Está causando furor.

He's all the rage.

He's at the height of fame.

Está en la cúspide de la fama.

Tiene el mundo a sus pies.

He has the world at his feet.

synonyms and similar words

célebre famous, celebrated
en boga in style
en la onda trendy, with it
  (*lit.*, in the sound wave)

actor (actriz) *m/f* actor/actress
celebridad *f* stardom; (a) celebrity
estrella *f* **de cine** movie star
estrella *f* **de televisión** TV star
farándula *f* show people, theater
  types

en primer plano in the limelight
famoso(-a) famous
favorito(-a) favorite
preferido(-a) favorite

ídolo *m* idol
rey (reina) *m/f* **de la noche**
  king/queen of the night
superestrella *f* superstar

related terms and expressions

estar en la cima de la fama to be at the height of fame
estar en la cresta de la ola to be riding high (*lit.*, be on the crest of the wave)
hacer brecha to break in, achieve fame
hacer furor to be all the rage
ser el centro de atención to be the center of attention
ser muy bien conocido(-a) to be very well known
ser número uno to be number one
ser todo un éxito (en la taquilla) to be a complete success (at the box
  office)
tener buena prensa to have a good reputation (*lit.*, good press)

Your mom looks a little uncomfortable, doesn't she?

Tu mamá se ve un poco incómoda, ¿verdad?

Cuando le presento a un nuevo amigo, no sabe dónde meterse.

When I introduce her to a new boyfriend, she doesn't know what to do with herself.

synonyms and similar words

apenado(-a) embarrassed
aprensivo(-a) apprehensive
avergonzado(-a) embarrassed
cohibido(-a) inhibited
desconcertado(-a) disconcerted

inquieto(-a) worried, restless
nervioso(-a) nervous
ruborizado(-a) blushing
tenso(-a) tense
vacilante hesitant

related terms and expressions

Ay, ¡trágame, tierra!	Oh, just kill me now! (*lit.*, Swallow me, earth!)
No está a gusto con gente desconocida.	He's ill at ease with strangers.
No sabe dónde meterse.	She doesn't know what to do with (*lit.*, where to put) herself.
Se avergüenza mucho.	She gets very embarrassed.
Se ruboriza.	She blushes.
Se siente como gallina en corral ajeno.	She feels like a fish out of water (*lit.*, a chicken in someone else's corral).
Se siente como gallo en patio ajeno.	He feels like a fish out of water (*lit.*, a rooster on someone else's patio).
Se siente muy cohibida.	She feels very inhibited.
Siente pena.	He feels embarrassed.
Trata de hacerse chiquita.	She tries to make herself very small.
Trata de hacerse invisible.	She tries to make herself invisible.

I read my newspaper cover to cover (lit., from end to tail) every day.

Todos los días leo el periódico de cabo a rabo.

Tienes que estar al corriente de las noticias.

You have to keep up with the news.

I like to stay informed, explore, consult the media, find out about everything ...

Me gusta mantenerme informado, explorar, consultar los medios de comunicación, enterarme de todo...

Hay que estar al día, informado y conectado.

You have to be up to date—informed and connected.

related terms and expressions

Estoy al corriente.	I'm up to date.
Estoy al día.	I'm up to date.
Estoy en el ajo.	I'm in the know (*lit.*, in the garlic).
Lo sé de buena tinta.	I have it on good authority (*lit.*, know it from good ink).
Tengo clara la película.	I get the picture. [Col, Peru, S Cone, Spain]
Todo me interesa.	Everything interests me.

averiguar algo to find something out
darse cuenta de algo to realize something
enterarse de algo to find out about something
fijarse en algo to notice something
informarse de algo to become informed about something
percatarse de algo to realize or notice something

opposites

Ignoraba la situación.	I didn't know about the situation.
Ignoraba que...	I didn't know that . . .
Me quedé a oscuras.	I was in the dark.
No estoy en nada.	I'm out of it. (*colloq.*)
No tenía la menor idea.	I had no idea.

ignorante ignorant, unaware

You've got lovely eyes, you know.

I can see you coming.

This fellow hits on (lit., *throws street compliments at*) every woman who goes by.

He's a real womanizer.

He's shameless.

That wolf tried to romance me last week.

synonyms and similar words

asaltacunas *m* cradle robber
buitre *m* wolf (*lit.*, vulture)
don Juan *m* Don Juan
mujeriego *m* womanizer
pulpo *m* guy who's all hands
 (*lit.*, octopus)

seductor(a) *m/f* seducer/seductress
tenorio *m* Don Juan
viejo(-a) *m/f* **verde** dirty old man/
 woman, letch

related terms and expressions

Es muy coqueto(-a).
Es un ligón.
Está cachondo(-a).
Está caliente.
¡Qué bombón y yo con diabetes!

¡Qué curvas y yo sin frenos!

abordar to make a pass at [Mex]
coquetear to flirt
echar los perros to hit on
 [Mex, C Am, S Am]
echar los tejos to hit on [Spain]
flirtear to flirt
hacer ojitos to make eyes at

He's/She's a real flirt.
He's a pick-up artist. [Col, Spain]
He's/She's horny. (*colloq.*)
She's hot. / He's turned on.
What a piece of candy, and me with
 diabetes!
What curves, and me without brakes!

levantarse a alguien to pick
 someone up [L Am]
ligar to pick up, make a conquest
tener una aventura to have a fling/
 affair
tirar los tejos to hit on [Spain]

Let's see how you did on the Personalidatos quiz (pages 38–40) and what it reveals about your personality!

25–34 Bravo! You're a great person: kind, considerate, generous, sociable. But it's time to think a bit less about others and a bit more about yourself: Charity begins at home!

35–42 You're a mixture of generosity and self-interest, with many good points that earn you lots of friends. You're the type that can get angry but then asks for forgiveness.

43–50 Well, you're not all that easy to live with: negative, inconsiderate, a bit anti-social, even grumpy. Learn to smile at others: If you don't do it for them, do it for yourself!

moods, emotions, and attitudes

mood swings

74 alert ~ tired 75
76 calm ~ anxious 77
78 cheerful ~ sad 79
80 encouraging ~ mocking 81
82 friendly ~ hostile 83
84 good reputation ~ bad reputation 85
86 happy ~ unhappy 87
88 passionate ~ indifferent 89
90 relieved ~ worried 91

Humorómetro 92

emotions and attitudes A~Z

amusement 95
anger 96
concentration 97
contempt 98
determination 99
disapproval 100
discouragement 101
embarrassment 102
fear 103
gratitude 104
health 105
hypocrisy 106
inspiration 107
jealousy 108
joy 109
laughter 110
satisfaction 111
sleep 112
suffering 113
surprise 114
touchiness 115
uncertainty 116
wonder 117

Humorómetro RESULTS 118

similar terms

astuto(-a) astute
atento(-a) attentive
avispado(-a) sharp, astute
cuidadoso(-a) careful
despejado(-a) clearheaded, alert
espabilado(-a) clearheaded, alert
reflexivo(-a) thoughtful
vigilante vigilant

atención *f* attention
concentración *f* concentration
conciencia *f* awareness
consideración *f* consideration
vigilancia *f* vigilance

common expressions

Camarón que se duerme se lo lleva la corriente. (REFRÁN)	Stay on your toes. (*lit.,* The shrimp that falls asleep is carried away by the current.)
¡Fíjate en eso!	Look at that!
¡Hay moros en la costa!	Be careful! (*lit.,* There are Moors on the coast!)
¡Hay ropa tendida!	Watch out! (*lit.,* There are clothes on the line!)
¡Hazme caso!	Pay attention to me!
¡Las paredes oyen!	The walls have ears (*lit.,* are listening)!
¡Levanta la antena!	Listen up! (*lit.,* Raise your antenna!)
¡Ojo!	Watch out! (*lit.,* Eye!)
¡Ojos abiertos!	Watch out! (*lit.,* Eyes open!)
¡Ponte mosca!	Keep your eyes peeled! (*lit.,* Make like a fly!)

enfocarse en lo más importante to focus on the essentials
escudriñar to scrutinize
estar bien despierto(-a) to be wide awake
estar con cien ojos to be on the lookout (*lit.,* to be with 100 eyes) [Spain]
estar con ojo to be on the lookout (*lit.,* to be with eye)
hacer algo con esmero to do something carefully
mantenerse a la defensiva to be on one's guard, be on the defensive
mantenerse con los ojos abiertos to keep one's eyes open
meter las narices en algo to stick one's nose into something
poner atención to pay attention
ponerse en guardia to be on one's guard
redoblar la atención to be twice as attentive
ser listo(-a) to be alert
vigilar to keep watch, be on the lookout

observador(a) *m/f* **atento(-a)** close observer

similar terms

agotado(-a) exhausted
amolado(-a) worn out, beat (*lit.*, ground down)
[Mex, C Am]
extenuado(-a) exhausted
fatigado(-a) tired
hecho(-a) pedazos worn to a frazzle (*lit.*, made
into pieces)
hecho(-a) pinole worn to a frazzle (*lit.*, made into
the fine powder used for making chocolate) [Mex]
hecho(-a) polvo worn to a frazzle (*lit.*, made into
dust)
hecho(-a) un puré worn to a frazzle (*lit.*, made
into a purée)
molido(-a) worn out, beat (*lit.*, ground down)
muerto(-a) de fatiga dead tired
quemado(-a) burned out
rendido(-a) worn out (*lit.*, rendered)
reventado(-a) worn out (*lit.*, cracked)
somnoliento(-a) drowsy

adormecimiento *m* drowsiness
agotamiento *m* exhaustion
cansancio *m* tiredness
fatiga *f* fatigue
lasitud *f* weariness
letargo *m* lethargy

modorra *f* drowsiness
pérdida *f* **de atención** inattentiveness
somnolencia *f* drowsiness
sopor *m* sleepiness
surmenaje *m* overwork, overexertion
torpeza *f* slowness, dullness

common expressions

Estoy que me caigo de sueño. I'm so sleepy I'm about to fall over.
Me duelen hasta los huesos. I'm bone tired. (*lit.*, Even my bones ache.)
Necesito planchar la oreja. I need to get some shut-eye
(*lit.*, iron my ear).
**No puedo mantenerme con
los ojos abiertos.** I can't keep my eyes open.
Tengo sueño. I'm sleepy.
Voy a meterme en el sobre. I'm going to put myself to bed
(*lit.*, in my envelope) [Ec, S Cone, Spain]

estar medio dormido(-a) to be half asleep
luchar contra el sueño to fight off sleep
quedarse sin fuerzas to be left with no energy

dormilón (dormilona) *m/f* sleepyhead

calm | calmado(-a)

Zen

similar terms

apacible gentle, mild
calmoso(-a) laid back, somewhat lazy
ecuánime even-tempered
impasible impassive, not emotional, unfeeling
plácido(-a) placid
relajado(-a) relaxed
sereno(-a) serene
tranquilo(-a) tranquil

confianza *f* confidence
paz *f* **interior** inner peace
quietud *f* tranquility
sangre *f* **fría** coolness under pressure
serenidad *f* serenity
tranquilidad *f* tranquility
tranquilidad *f* **de espíritu** peace of mind

common expressions

Cálmate.	Calm down.
Conserva una calma olímpica.	She maintains a godly calm.
Es de carácter calmado.	He has a calm character.
Es de carácter pacífico.	He has a peaceful character.
Mantiene su equilibrio; es una persona equilibrada.	He keeps his equilibrium; he's an even-tempered person.
No es para tanto.	It's no big deal. / It's not that important.
No te hagas mala sangre.	Don't get upset. (*lit.*, Don't make bad blood for yourself.)
No te sofoques.	Don't get steamed.
No te sulfures.	Don't get steamed.
Toma las cosas con calma.	Take life as it comes. (*lit.*, Take things calmly.)
Tranquilízate.	Calm down.
Tranquilo.	Calm down.

controlar las emociones to control one's emotions
ser dueño(-a) de sí mismo(-a) to be self-controlled, in possession of oneself

¡Ay, ay, ay!

similar terms

aprensivo(-a) apprehensive
asustadizo(-a) easily frightened
desconcertado(-a) disconcerted
estresado(-a) stressed out (*colloq.*)
friqueado(-a) freaked out (*colloq.*) [Mex, Carib]
miedoso(-a) fearful
preocupado(-a) worried
temeroso(-a) fearful
tenso(-a) tense

agitación *f* agitation
angustia *f* anguish
ansiedad *f* anxiety
ataque *m* **de nervios** attack of nerves, stage fright
congoja *f* distress, anxiety
crisis *f* **nerviosa** nervous breakdown
inquietud *f* disquiet, worry
intranquilidad *f* uneasiness
miedo *m* fear
nerviosismo *m* nervousness
preocupación *f* worry
tensión *f* tension
turbación *f* embarrassment, perturbation
zozobra *f* anxiety

common expressions

Estoy en ascuas.	I'm on pins and needles (*lit.*, embers).
Me dan ñáñaras.	I get the willies. [Mex, parts of C Am]
Me muerdo las uñas.	I bite my nails.
Me siento inseguro(-a).	I feel insecure.
Me siento muy nervioso(-a).	I feel very nervous.
Tengo el alma en un hilo.	I'm a bundle of nerves. (*lit.*, I have my soul on a thread.)
Tengo el corazón en un puño.	I'm a nervous wreck. (*lit.*, I have my heart in a fist.)
Tengo los nervios de punta.	My nerves are on edge.
Tengo un nudo en la garganta.	I have a lump (*lit.*, knot) in my throat.

¡Qué alegría!

similar terms

animado(-a) lively
contento(-a) glad
dinámico(-a) dynamic, energetic
encantado(-a) delighted
jovial merry, jovial
juguetón (juguetona) playful
radiante beaming, radiant
regocijado(-a) delighted
risueño(-a) cheerful, smiling
sonriente smiling

alegría *f* happiness
capricho *m* whim
encanto *m* enchantment
euforia *f* euphoria
felicidad *f* bliss, happiness
jovialidad *f* joviality
júbilo *m* joy
placer *m* pleasure
regocijo *m* joy, delight

common expressions

¡Bacán!	Super! / Great! [Cuba, Col, Ec, Peru, S Cone]
¡Buenos días a todos! ¡Qué alegría verlos!	Hello, everyone! How happy I am to see you!
¡Chévere!	Super! / Great! [Carib, Ven, Col]
Estoy de buen ánimo.	I'm in good spirits.
Estoy de muy buen humor.	I'm in a great mood.
Estoy en la gloria.	I'm in seventh heaven.
La vida me sonríe.	Life is beautiful (*lit.*, smiling at me).
¡Qué guay!	Super! / Great! [Spain]
¡Qué padre!	Super! / Great! [Mex]
¡Regio!	Super! / Great! [Nic, Col, Ec, S Cone]
Todo anda sobre ruedas.	Everything is going smoothly (*lit.*, on wheels).
Todo lo veo color de rosa.	I see everything through rose-colored glasses.
Todo va requetebién.	Everything is going super.
¡Tuanis!	Super! / Great! [CR]

dar saltos de alegría to jump for joy
estar alegre como unas castañuelas to be happy as a clam (*lit.*, as castanets)
estar como niño con zapatos nuevos to be like a kid in a candy store (*lit.*, with new shoes)
estar encantado(-a) de la vida to be happy as can be (*lit.*, enchanted with life)
tener una sonrisa de oreja a oreja to be smiling ear to ear

¡Qué bajón!

similar terms

abatido(-a) despondent
acongojado(-a) distressed
afligido(-a) afflicted, distressed
deprimido(-a) depressed
desconsolado(-a) disconsolate
desilusionado(-a) disillusioned
melancólico(-a) morose, sad
sombrío(-a) somber

aflicción *f* affliction
angustia *f* distress, anguish
depresión *f* depression
desaliento *m* discouragement
lloriqueo *m* whining
pena *f* sadness
pesadumbre *f* sorrow
tristeza *f* sorrow

common expressions

El gozo en un pozo.	It's all down the drain. (*lit.*, The pleasure in a well.)
Es deplorable.	It's deplorable.
Es fatal.	It's awful (*lit.*, fatal).
Es lamentable.	It's lamentable.
Es patético(-a).	It's pathetic.
Está por el suelo.	It's the pits (*lit.*, on the floor).
Estoy al punto de llorar.	I'm on the verge of tears.
He tocado fondo.	I'm at rock bottom.
¡Qué bajón!	What a bummer!
¡Qué tristeza!	How pathetic!
Se me cayó el alma a los pies.	I lost heart. (*lit.*, My soul fell to my feet.)
Tengo una depre.	I'm feeling blue. (*lit.*, I have a depression.)
Todo lo veo negro.	Everything looks bleak. (*lit.*, I see everything black.)

llorar a mares to cry buckets (*lit.*, seas)
ser como alma en pena to be like a soul in torment

el caballero de la triste figura (don Quijote) the knight with the sad countenance (Don Quixote)

caralarga *m/f* sad sack (*lit.*, long face)

¡Bravo!

similar terms

dinámico(-a) dynamic
esperanzador(a) encouraging, giving hope
positivo(-a) positive

aplauso *m* applause
apoyo *m* support
aprobación *f* approval
cumplido *m* compliment
elogio *m* praise
estímulo *m* stimulus
incentivo *m* incentive

common expressions

¡Al agua, patos! — Let's go! / Let's do it! (*lit.*, To the water, ducks!)

¡Ánimo! — Hang in there!

¡Así se hace! — Way to go!

¡Aupa! — Go! (*sports event*) [Spain]

¡Bravo! ¡Muy bien! ¡Excelente! — Bravo! Great! Excellent!

¡Échale ganas! — Put your heart in it!

¡Felicitaciones! — Congratulations!

¡Órale! — All right! / That's it! [Mex, parts of C Am]

¡Puedes hacerlo! ¡Ten confianza en ti mismo(-a)! — You can do it! Believe in yourself!

alentar to encourage
animar to encourage, cheer/brighten up
darle alas a alguien to encourage someone (*lit.*, give someone wings)
darle confianza a alguien to reassure someone, give someone confidence
darle marcha a alguien to give someone energy / a boost / a lift [Spain]
elogiar to praise
esperanzar to give hope
estimular to stimulate
exhortar to exhort
ilusionar to build up (someone's) hopes
inspirar to inspire
levantar el ánimo a alguien to boost someone's morale, raise spirits
motivar to motivate
rendir homenaje a alguien to pay homage to someone

similar terms

crítico(-a) critical
fresco(-a) fresh, sassy
grosero(-a) rude
insolente insolent
irónico(-a) ironic
malicioso(-a) malicious
ofensivo(-a) insulting
sarcástico(-a) sarcastic

broma *f* joke
burla *m* scoff, jeer
chiste *m* joke
farsa *f* hoax, farce
ocurrencia *f* funny or interesting thing that occurs to someone,
  witty remark
pulla *f* cutting remark
puntada *f* wisecrack [Mex, parts of C Am]
salida *f* wisecrack, cutting remark
sarcasmo *m* sarcasm
sátira *f* satire

common expressions

burlarse de alguien to make fun of someone
cachondearse de alguien to tease someone, make fun of someone [Spain]
echar indirectas to make jibes
hacer una broma de mal gusto to play a trick or make a joke that is
  in bad taste
hacer una broma pesada to play a trick or make a joke that is unpleasant
mofarse de to mock, jeer
poner en ridículo a alguien to make fun of someone
ridiculizar to make fun of, ridicule
ser el hazmerreír to be the laughingstock
tomarle el pelo a alguien to put someone on, pull someone's leg (*lit.*, hair)
vacilar to tease, make fun of, kid

bromista *m/f* joker, prankster
caricatura *f* caricature
doble sentido *m* double meaning
ironía *f* irony

friendly | amable

¿Qué tal?

similar terms

abierto(-a) open
agradable agreeable, pleasant
amigable friendly
amistoso(-a) friendly
amoroso(-a) loving
atento(-a) caring, attentive
cálido(-a) warm
cariñoso(-a) affectionate
complaciente accommodating
cordial cordial
cortés polite, courteous
ecuánime easygoing
extrovertido(-a) outgoing
gregario(-a) gregarious
simpático(-a) nice, pleasant
sociable sociable

amabilidad *f* friendliness
bondad *f* kindness
calor *m* **humano** warmth
cariño *m* affection
cordialidad *f* cordiality
cortesía *f* politeness, courtesy
sociabilidad *f* sociability

common expressions

Es el mejor de los mejores (la mejor de las mejores).	He's/She's the best.
Es un verdadero amigo (una verdadera amiga).	He's/She's a real friend.
Los buenos amigos son difíciles de encontrar, más difíciles de dejar e imposibles de olvidar. (REFRÁN)	Good friends are hard to find, harder to leave behind, and impossible to forget.
Siempre está para servir a los amigos.	She's always there for her friends.

cole *m/f* colleague, pal
compadre (comadre) *m/f* very close friend who is sometimes a godparent to one's child [L Am]
compañero(-a) *m/f* friend
compinche *m/f* friend, pal [L Am]
cuate(-a) *m/f* friend [Mex]
pana *m/f* friend [Carib, Col, Ven, Ec]

similar terms

antipático(-a) unpleasant
belicoso(-a) bellicose
colérico(-a) given to anger
desagradable unpleasant
gruñón (gruñona) grumpy
irritable irritable
odioso(-a) hateful
pendenciero(-a) quarrelsome
pleitista given to fighting
reñidor(a) quarrelsome
repugnante repulsive
vindicativo(-a) vindictive

animosidad *f* animosity
hostilidad *f* hostility
odio *m* hatred
repulsión *f* repulsion

¡GRR!

common expressions

Estamos peleados.	We've fallen out. / We've quarreled.
Estoy hasta la coronilla con ella.	I've had it up to here (*lit.*, to the crown) with her.
La detesto.	I detest her.
Me cae mal.	I don't like him.
No la puedo ver ni pintada.	I can't stand the sight of her.
No la soporto.	I can't stand her.
No la trago.	I can't stand her.
No lo puedo ver ni en pintura.	I can't stand the sight of him.
No lo tolero.	I can't stand him.
Nos grita a todos.	He yells at all of us.
¡Qué carácter más pesado! Tiene muy mal carácter.	What a bad disposition! He has a bad disposition.

abominar to loathe
detestar to despise, detest

similar terms

Para tener buena reputación, hay que ser...
To have a good reputation, you've got
to be ...
amoroso(-a) loving
bondadoso(-a) kind
bueno(-a) en todos los aspectos
good in every respect
cortés polite
decente decent
derecho(-a) upstanding
escrupuloso(-a) scrupulous
ético(-a) ethical
fiel faithful
generoso(-a) generous
honesto(-a) honest
honrado(-a) honorable
justo(-a) fair
leal loyal
modesto(-a) modest
productivo(-a) productive
respetado(-a) en la comunidad
respected in the community
sensible sensitive
servicial helpful
sincero(-a) sincere
trabajador(a) hardworking

common expressions

A todo el mundo le cae bien.	Everyone likes him.
Es muy buena gente.	She is a good person.
Es muy buena onda.	He is a good egg.
Es un amor.	He is a peach (*lit.*, love).
Es un ángel.	She is an angel.
Es una joya.	She is a gem.
"Más vale el buen nombre que las muchas riquezas." (Miguel de Cervantes)	"A good name is better than many riches."
Nunca hizo mal a nadie.	He never hurt a fly (*lit.*, never hurt anyone).
Su conducta es intachable.	Her behavior is beyond reproach.
Tiene fama de ser honesto y serio, sin pretensiones.	He has a reputation for being honest and serious, without pretense.
Tiene las manos limpias.	He has a clean past (*lit.*, hands).

¡GRRR!

similar terms

brutal brutal
cruel cruel
descortés rude
deshonesto(-a) dishonest
egoísta selfish
malicioso(-a) malicious
obsesionado(-a) obsessed
perezoso(-a) lazy
pretensioso(-a) pretentious
repugnante disgusting
sanguinario(-a) bloodthirsty
sin corazón heartless
tacaño(-a) stingy
violento(-a) violent

aprovechado(-a) *m/f* opportunist
asesino(-a) *m/f* murderer
delator(a) *m/f* squealer, informer
estafador(a) *m/f* crook
explotador(a) *m/f* user, exploiter
gángster *m/f* gangster
ladrón (ladrona) *m/f* thief
mafioso(-a) *m/f* thug, mafioso
matón (matona) *m/f* thug, bully

perverso(-a) *m/f* evil or wicked person
racista *m/f* racist
sádico(-a) *m/f* sadist
terrorista *m/f* terrorist
tirano(-a) *m/f* tyrant
torturador(a) *m/f* torturer
traficante *m/f* trafficker
violador(a) *m/f* rapist

common expressions

Dios los cría y ellos se juntan. (REFRÁN)
God creates them and they get together.

Dios sufre a los malos, pero no para siempre. (REFRÁN)
God puts up with bad people, but not forever.

◑ **Es un hijo de su.**
He's a son of a gun.

Es un verdadero sinvergüenza.
He's a real scumbag.

Es una manzana podrida.
She's a rotten apple.

¡Este tipo es un descarado!
This guy's a jerk!

tener mala fama to have a bad name

◑ **banda** *f* **de cabrones** bunch of bad asses
calzonazos *m* wimp [Spain]
calzonudo *m* wimp
cerdo(-a) *m/f* pig
cochino(-a) *m/f* pig
holgazán (holgazana) *m/f* lazy bum

macarras *mpl* bad guys [Spain]
malvados *mpl* bad guys
opresor(a) *m/f* oppressor
◑ **pandilla** *f* **de cabrones** bunch of bad asses
sinvergüenza *m/f* scum, jerk (*lit.*, shameless person)
vagabundo(-a) *m/f* bum

¡Hurra!

similar terms

afortunado(-a) fortunate
alegre merry, happy
contento(-a) glad
dichoso(-a) fortunate, lucky
encantado(-a) delighted
satisfecho(-a) satisfied
sereno(-a) serene

alborozo *m* jubilation, joy
encanto *m* enchantment, charm
felicidad *f* bliss
júbilo *m* joy
placer *m* pleasure

common expressions

Desgraciado(-a) en el juego, afortunado(-a) en amores.	Unlucky at gambling, lucky in love.
Estoy como pez en el agua.	I'm in my element (*lit.,* like a fish in water).
Estoy en la gloria.	I'm in seventh heaven.
"La felicidad, a semejanza del arte, cuanto más se calcula, menos se logra." (Enrique Jardiel Poncela)	"Happiness, like art, is least obtained the more it is calculatingly sought."
La vida me sonríe.	Life is beautiful (*lit.,* smiling at me).
Soy alegre como unas castañuelas.	I'm happy as a clam (*lit.,* castanets).
Soy feliz como una lombriz.	I'm happy as a clam (*lit.,* worm).
Todo anda sobre ruedas.	Everything is going smoothly (*lit.,* on wheels).
Todo lo veo color de rosa.	I see everything through rose-colored glasses.

¡Lástima!

similar terms

afligido(-a) afflicted, troubled
castigado(-a) stricken, punished
desafortunado(-a) unfortunate
desgraciado(-a) unlucky
destrozado(-a) devastated
lamentable pitiful
patético(-a) pathetic
pobre poor
triste sad

accidente *m* accident
adversidad *f* adversity
azote *m* scourge
calamidad *f* calamity, misfortune
contratiempo *m* setback
desastre *m* disaster
desgracia *f* misfortune
dolor *m* pain, grief
fatalidad *f* casualty, fatality
fracaso *m* failure
golpe *m* **duro** setback, hard blow
luto *m* mourning
mala suerte *f* bad luck

pena *f* sorrow
pérdida *f* loss
plaga *f* blight, menace, plague
prueba *f* hardship
revés *m* reversal (of fortune), setback
ruina *f* ruin
tragedia *f* tragedy

common expressions

Después de la lluvia, sale el sol.
(REFRÁN)

Every cloud has a silver lining.
(*lit.,* After the rain, the sun comes out.)

Es gafe.
He's a jinx. [Spain]

Ha sufrido algunos percances.
She's suffered some mishaps.

Las desgracias nunca vienen solas. (REFRÁN)
It never rains but it pours.
(*lit.,* Misfortunes never come one at a time.)

Llueve sobre mojado. (REFRÁN)
It's one bad thing after another.
(*lit.,* It's raining over wetness.)

Lo ve todo negro.
Everything looks bleak to him.
(*lit.,* He sees everything black.)

Pobre de él.
Poor guy.

¡Qué perra vida!
What a bitch of a life!

¡Qué vida de perros!
What a bitch of a life!

Su vida es una telenovela.
Her life is a soap opera.

Unos nacen con estrella y otros nacen estrellados. (REFRÁN)
Some people are born with a lucky star and others are born shattered.

¡Me encanta!

similar terms

ardiente ardent
comprometido(-a) committed, engaged
emocionado(-a) thrilled, excited
enamorado(-a) in love
enardecido(-a) fired up
entusiasta enthusiastic
fanático(-a) fanatical, enthusiastic
ferviente devoted, fervent
frenético(-a) frantic, frenetic
impetuoso(-a) impetuous
loco(-a) por wild about

entusiasmo *m* enthusiasm
fanatismo *m* fanaticism
pasión *f* **por algo** passion for something

common expressions

Es un amor incondicional.	It's unconditional love.
Es un apoyo incondicional.	It's unconditional support.
Le entusiasma todo.	She's enthusiastic about everything.
Te amo. Te quiero mucho.	I love you. I love you very much.
Te adoro.	I adore you.

adorar to adore, love
anhelar mucho to be eager, be zealous
emocionarse to get excited
enardecerse to get fired up
exaltarse to get worked up, get excited

apasionadamente passionately
con ardor passionately
con furia furiously
locamente madly, in a crazy way

adepto(-a) *m/f* follower, devotee
admirador(a) *m/f* admirer
aficionado(-a) *m/f* fan
discípulo(-a) *m/f* disciple, follower
forofo(-a) *m/f* (sports) fan [Spain]
hincha *m/f* (sports) fan
partidario(-a) *m/f* follower, supporter

similar terms

apático(-a) apathetic
desdeñoso(-a) scornful
duro(-a) hard
estoico(-a) stoic
frío(-a) cold
hastiado(-a) jaded
impasible impassive, unemotional
imperturbable imperturbable
insensible insensitive

corazón *m* **de piedra** heart of stone
desenvoltura *f* offhand manner, casualness
despreocupación *f* lack of concern
dureza *f* hardness, harshness
indiferencia *f* indifference
insensibilidad *f* insensitivity

common expressions

Es una persona seca.	He's an unemotional (*lit.*, dry) person.
Gran cosota.	Big deal (*lit.*, thing).
Me da igual.	It's all the same to me.
Me da lo mismo.	It's all the same to me.
Me importa un pepino/comino/ rábano/bledo.	I don't give a darn (*lit.*, a cucumber / cumin seed / radish / pigweed).
◑ Me importan tres cojones.	I don't give a damn. (*lit.*, It's as important to me as three testicles.) [Spain]
◑ Me la suda.	I don't give a damn.
◑ Me vale madre.	I don't give a damn. [Mex, C Am]
Ni me va ni me viene.	It doesn't matter to me. / I could take it or leave it. (*lit.*, It doesn't go or come to me.)
No es mi problema.	It's not my problem.
No me hace ni fu ni fa.	It doesn't matter to me. / I could take it or leave it. (*lit.*, It doesn't do fu or fa for me.)
No me interesa en lo más mínimo.	It doesn't interest me in the least.
¿Qué más da?	Who cares? (*lit.*, What more does it give?) [L Am]

¡Uf!

similar terms

calmado(-a) relaxed
consolado(-a) consoled
relajado(-a) relaxed
sereno(-a) serene
tranquilizado(-a) consoled

consuelo *m* consolation
desahogo *m* unburdening, venting
descarga *f* **(de emociones)** release
  (of emotions)
mejoría *f* improvement
relajación *f* relaxation
relajamiento *m* relaxation, loosening (up)

common expressions

¡Cuánto me alegro!	I'm so happy!
¡Fue mano de santo!	It was a sure cure (*lit.*, saint's hand)!
¡Gracias a Dios!	Thank God!
¡Justo a tiempo!	At last! / Just in time!
¡Me salvé por un pelo!	I was saved by a hair!
¡Menos mal!	Just as well!
Necesito desahogarme con alguien.	I need to vent to someone.
¡Por fin! ¡Qué suerte!	Finally! What luck!
¡Qué alivio!	What a relief!
¡Tanto mejor!	So much the better!
¡Veo la luz al final del túnel!	I see the light at the end of the tunnel!
¡Ya estamos!	We're there! / We're done!

aliviar to relieve, lighten
desahogarse to unburden oneself, vent
liberarle a alguien de una carga to relieve someone of a burden/
  responsibility
mejorarse to get better, improve
quitarse un peso de encima to take a load off
recuperarse to recuperate

¡Ay, ay, ay!

similar terms

ansioso(-a) anxious
aprensivo(-a) apprehensive
desconcertado(-a) disconcerted
estresado(-a) stressed out (*colloq.*)
miedoso(-a) fearful
preocupado(-a) worried
tenso(-a) tense

agitación *f* agitation
alarma *f* alarm
angustia *f* **existencial** existentialist angst
ansiedad *f* **profunda** deep anxiety
congoja *f* distress, anxiety
fobia *f* phobia
inquietud *f* concern, worry
miedos *mpl* fears
opresión *f* oppression

pánico *m* panic
preocupación *f* worry
tormento *m* torment
zozobra *f* anxiety

common expressions

Estoy al punto de hundirme.	I'm about to crack (*lit.*, sink).
Estoy en ascuas.	I'm on pins and needles (*lit.*, embers).
Estoy estresado(-a).	I'm stressed out.
Me muerdo las uñas.	I bite my nails.
No pegué los ojos en toda la noche.	I didn't close (*lit.*, glue shut) my eyes all night.
No puedo relajarme.	I can't relax.
Pasé la noche en vela.	I spent the night wide awake (*lit.*, on watch).
Tengo el alma en un hilo.	I'm a bundle of nerves. (*lit.*, I have my soul on a thread.)
Tengo el corazón en un puño.	I'm a nervous wreck. (*lit.*, I have my heart in a fist.)
Tengo los nervios de punta.	My nerves are on edge.
¡Tengo miedo!	I'm scared!
Tengo un nudo en la garganta.	I have a lump (*lit.*, knot) in my throat.

ceder al pánico to give way to panic
dar canas to give gray hair
tener sudores fríos to break out in a cold sweat

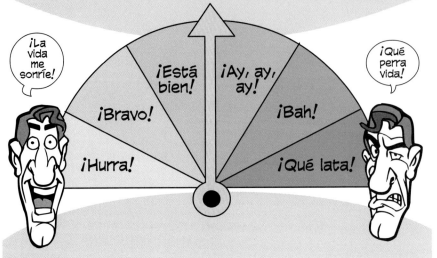

Humorómetro

How emotional are you? For each of the following situations, choose (a) or (b), based on how you would probably feel. Depending on your answer, you earn one or two points. If you need help, follow the cross-reference to the page(s) indicated. Answer the questions and add up your score.

1 • You're at the movies watching a thriller after an exhausting day at work. ☞ 74–75
   a Estás medio dormido(-a); no puedes mantenerte con los ojos abiertos. (1)
   b Estás muy atento(-a); el suspense te está matando. (2)

2 • You have to give a speech in front of a large audience. ☞ 76–77
   a Eres dueño(-a) de ti mismo(-a). (1)
   b Tienes los nervios de punta. (2)

3 • You lose your passport and wallet while traveling. ☞ 76–77
   a Tienes el alma en un hilo. (2)
   b Tomas las cosas con calma. (1)

4 • You're thinking about your childhood. ☞ 78–79
   a Lo ves todo color de rosa. (1)
   b Estás al punto de llorar. (2)

5 • You're reminiscing about your first sweetheart. ☞ 78–79
   a Tienes una sonrisa de oreja a oreja. (1)
   b Se te cae el alma a los pies. (2)

6 • You're playing tennis and you hit the ball high over the fence. ☞ 80–81
   a Te sientes el hazmerreír de todos. (2)
   b Te ríes y te animas a seguir con el partido. (1)

7 • New neighbors move in next door. ☞ 82–83
   a Te presentas cordialmente. (1)
   b Ni los saludas porque te caen mal. (2)

8 • You lose your iPod. ☞ 86–87
   a Vas a la tienda y compras otro. (1)
   b Te parece una calamidad. Estás destrozado(-a). (2)

9 • Your home team is losing the game. ☞ 88–89
   a Te emocionas mucho; tratas de animar a los jugadores. (2)
   b Ni te va ni te viene. (1)

10 • During a flight the child next to you spills cranberry juice on your shirt. ☞ 96
   a Pierdes los estribos y le insultas. (2)
   b No le dices nada. (1)

11 • You arrive at a hotel and they don't have a room for you even though you made a reservation weeks in advance. ☞ 96
   a Te quejas cortésmente con el gerente. (1)
   b Te pones como una fiera. (2)

12 • You're passed over for a raise. ☞ 101
   a Estás al punto de hundirte. (2)
   b Decides hablar otra vez con tu jefe. (1)

13 • You forget your boss' name suddenly while introducing him at a formal meeting. ☞ 102
   a Te ríes y le pides perdón. (1)
   b Te pones como un tomate y no sabes dónde meterte. (2)

14 • You're walking along an obscure street and you come to a cemetery. ☞ 103
   a Se te pone la carne de gallina. (2)
   b Sigues caminando como si nada. (1)

15 • You hear a noise at the front of your house and think there is a robber trying to get in. ☞ 103
   a Das diente con diente y te quedas inmóvil. (2)
   b Te levantas para ir a ver qué pasa. (1)

16 • A nice guy returns a suitcase that you had lost. ☞ 104
   a Te sientes muy agradecido(-a). (2)
   b No agradeces nada. (1)

17 • Your best friend buys a Mercedes. ☞ 108
   a Lo llamas y lo felicitas. (1)
   b Te pones muerto(-a) de envidia. (2)

18 • You win the lottery. ☞ 109
    a Estallas de júbilo y das saltos de alegría. (2)
    b Empiezas a pensar en todos los impuestos que habrá que pagar. (1)

19 • Someone plays a practical joke on you. ☞ 110
    a Carcajeas y te ríes a lo loco. (1)
    b No te parece chistoso. (2)

20 • You visit your mother in the hospital. ☞ 113
    a Te parte el alma verla sufrir. (2)
    b No le dedicas mucho tiempo; te vas después de diez minutos. (1)

To see how you did on the Humorómetro, turn to page 118.

¡Je je!

similar terms

distracción *f* amusement; distraction
entretenimiento *m* entertainment
pasatiempo *m* pastime
ratos *mpl* **libres** free time
recreo *m* recreation

common expressions

Ellos sí saben divertirse.	They sure know how to have fun.
¡Es una pachanga de primera clase!	It's a real (*lit.*, first-class) bash!
¡Qué divertido!	What fun!
¡Qué fiesta más animada!	What a great (*lit.*, lively) party!
Son fiesteros.	They're party animals.
Son parrandistas.	They're party animals.

darse la buena vida to live it up
divertirse to have fun
hacer el viacrucis to go barhopping (*lit.*, to do the stations of the cross) [Spain]
ir de juerga to go out on the town
ir de marcha to go out on the town [Spain]
ir de parranda to go out on the town
ir de paseo to go for a ride/stroll
pasarla de película to have a great time
pasarlo bomba to have a great time [S Cone, Spain]
pasarlo en grande to have a great time [Spain]
pasarlo (pasarla) bien to have a good time
pasear to go for a ride/stroll
relajarse to relax
salir de marcha to go out on the town [Spain]
trasnochar to stay up late or stay out all night

día *m* **de fiesta** holiday
farra *f* bash, party [Ec, S Cone, Spain]
festival *m* festival
fiesta *f* party
hobby *m* hobby
pachanga *f* bash, party
reventón *m* bash, party [Mex, C Am]

similar terms

enojo *m* anger
furia *f* fury
ira *f* anger, ire
rabia *f* rage

bravo(-a) angry [L Am]
colérico(-a) short-tempered
enfadado(-a) angry
enfurecido(-a) furious
enojado(-a) angry
exasperado(-a) exasperated
furioso(-a) furious
irascible irascible
irritable irritable

common expressions

Estoy como agua para chocolate.	I'm at the boiling point (*lit.*, like water for chocolate). [Mex]
Estoy como todos los diablos.	I'm beside myself (*lit.*, like all the devils). [Mex, C Am]
◑ Estoy hasta los cojones.	I'm really pissed off (*lit.*, up to my balls).
Estoy que se me lleva el demonio.	I'm about to blow my lid. (*lit.*, I'm ready for the devil to take me.)
Hice un berrinche.	I had a fit.
Me hace hervir la sangre.	It makes my blood boil.
Me salí de las casillas.	I'm totally unhinged (*lit.*, went out of my little boxes).
Perdí los estribos.	I lost my cool (*lit.*, the stirrups).
Se me fue la olla.	I lost it. (*lit.*, The pot went away from me.) [Spain]
Se me subió la mostaza.	I lost my temper. (*lit.*, Mustard went up on me.)

◑ **cabrearse** to get pissed off [Mex, Spain]
echar chispas/humo/rayos to be steamed (*lit.*, to let off sparks / smoke / lightning bolts)
◑ **encabronarse** to get pissed off [most of L Am]
estar fastidiado(-a)/molesto(-a)/picado(-a) to be annoyed
explotar to explode
hacer una pataleta/rabieta to have a fit, throw a tantrum
ponerse como una fiera to go wild, become like a wild beast
sofocarse to get upset, get angry
sulfurarse to blow one's top

enojón (enojona) *m/f* hothead
fosforito *m/f* hothead (*lit.*, little match) [parts of L Am]

similar terms

atención *f* attention
conciencia *f* conscience
contemplación *f* contemplation
entendimiento *m* understanding
inteligencia *f* intelligence
introspección *f* introspection
meditación *f* meditation
mente *f* mind
pensamiento *m* **profundo** deep thought
razón *f* reason
reflexión *f* reflection
vida *f* **interior** inner life

common expressions

Eso te hace pensar.	It makes you think.
Estás usando el coco.	You're using your noggin (*lit.*, coconut).
Hay que pesar los pros y los contras.	You have to weigh the pros and cons.
Pensándolo bien...	On second thought (*lit.*, thinking it over well) ...
Piénsalo en serio.	Think about it seriously.
Tienes que concentrarte.	You have to concentrate.
Usa la cabeza.	Use your head.

contemplar to contemplate
devanarse los sesos to rack one's brain
enfocar to focus
especular to speculate
juzgar to judge, consider
meditar to meditate
preguntarse to wonder (about)
razonar to reason
reflexionar intensamente (sobre) to think intently (about)
romperse la cabeza to think hard (*lit.*, break one's head)
soñar to dream, daydream

contempt | el desprecio

similar terms

altanería *f* condescension, arrogance
altivez *f* haughtiness
arrogancia *f* arrogance
desdén *m* disdain
indiferencia *f* indifference
soberbia *f* pride

arrogante arrogant
creído(-a) stuck-up
despreciable despicable
engreído(-a) stuck-up
orgulloso(-a) proud
presumido(-a) conceited, presumptuous
soberbio(-a) proud

common expressions

La odio.	I hate her.
Me mira por encima del hombro.	She looks down her nose (*lit.*, shoulder) at me.
Me miró de pie a cabeza.	He looked me up and down (*lit.*, from foot to head).
Me ninguneó.	He treated me like dirt (*lit.*, like a nobody).
No me llega a la suela del zapato.	She can't hold a candle to me (*lit.*, doesn't come up to the sole of my shoe).
○ ¡Que se vaya a la mierda!	Screw him! (*lit.*, May he go to shit!)
○ ¡Que se vaya al infierno!	Screw her! (*lit.*, May she go to hell!)
Se burló de mí.	He made fun of me.
Se cree mucho.	She thinks she's the cat's meow. (*lit.*, She thinks a lot of herself.)
Se rió de mí.	He laughed at me.

fantasioso(-a) *m/f* show-off; *adj* stuck-up
fantoche *m/f* show-off; *adj* stuck-up
pretensioso(-a) *m/f* show-off; *adj* pretentious

la determinación — determination

similar terms

autodeterminación *f* self-determination
decisión *f* decision
motivación *f* motivation
obstinación *f* obstinacy
persistencia *f* persistence
resolución *f* resolution
tenacidad *f* tenacity
terquedad *f* stubbornness
testarudez *f* stubbornness

cabezón (cabezona) pigheaded, stubborn
caprichoso(-a) willful, impulsive
firme firm
obstinado(-a) obstinate
tenaz tenacious, persistent
terco(-a) stubborn
testarudo(-a) headstrong
tozudo(-a) stubborn

common expressions

Estoy resuelto(-a); no hay vuelta de hoja.
I'm resolved; there's no turning back (*lit.*, no turning of the page).

Me mantengo en mis trece.
I'm sticking to my guns (*lit.*, staying in my thirteen).

Me quedaré firme hasta el final.
I'll hold out till the bitter end.

No daré mi brazo a torcer.
I won't give up. (*lit.*, I won't give my arm to twist.)

No me daré por vencido(-a).
I won't give up.

No me doy.
I won't give in.

No me rindo.
I won't give in.

No voy a tirar la toalla.
I won't throw in the towel.

¡Qué va!

similar terms

condenación *f* condemnation
crítica *f* criticism
culpa *f* blame
desacuerdo *m* disagreement
moción *f* **de censura** vote of no confidence
rechazo *m* rejection
reproche *m* reproach

common expressions

¡De ninguna manera!	No way!
¡Es inútil!	It's useless!
¡Es totalmente inaceptable!	It's totally unacceptable!
¡Es una locura!	It's crazy!
¡Ni a palos!	No way! (*lit.*, Not even by blows!)
¡Ni en sueños!	Not in your dreams!
¡Ni loco(-a)!	No way! (*lit.*, Not even crazy!)
¡Ni pensarlo!	Don't even think about it!
¡No estoy de acuerdo!	I disagree!
¡No lo podemos tolerar!	We can't tolerate it!
¡No sirve!	It's no good! (*lit.*, It doesn't serve!)
¡Qué tonterías!	Nonsense!
¡Qué va!	Oh, come on!
¡Va en contra de mis principios!	It goes against my principles!

condenar to condemn
criticar to criticize
desaprobar to disapprove
echar la culpa to blame
fruncir el ceño to frown
rechazar to reject
regañar to scold
reprobar to condemn, disapprove
reprochar to reproach

¡Bah!

similar terms

abatimiento *m* dejection
angustia *f* distress, anguish
decaimiento *m* fall into a state of weakness
   or discouragement
derrota *f* defeat
desaliento *m* discouragement
desengaño *m* realization of the truth,
   disillusionment
desesperación *f* desperation
desesperanza *f* despair, hopelessness
fiasco *m* fiasco
fracaso *m* failure
ilusiones *fpl* **perdidas** lost illusions
pérdida *f* **de moral** loss of morale
sorpresa *f* **desagradable** unpleasant surprise

abatido(-a) disheartened
arrepentido(-a) contrite
compungido(-a) distressed, remorseful
decepcionado(-a) disappointed

deprimido(-a) depressed
desalentado(-a) discouraged
desanimado(-a) discouraged

common expressions

El gozo en un pozo.
   It's a bummer. (*lit.,* The pleasure in a
   well.)

Ⓞ Está jodido.
   It's all screwed up.

Estoy al punto de hundirme.
   I'm about to crack (*lit.,* sink).

Fui por lana y volví
   trasquilado(-a).
   I had the tables turned on me. (*lit.,* I
   went for wool and came back shorn.)

Ⓞ La cagué.
   I screwed up (*lit.,* shit it).

Me doy por vencido(-a).
   I give up.

No veo la luz al final del túnel.
   I don't see the light at the end of the
   tunnel.

¡Qué bajón!
   What a downer!

Tengo el rabo entre las piernas.
   I've got my tail between my legs.

Tengo una depre.
   I've got the blues.

abandonar to give up, abandon
abatir to dishearten
apearse/bajarse del burro to give in (*lit.,* to get off the donkey)
bajar las orejas to give in (*lit.,* to lower one's ears)
capitular to capitulate
deprimir to depress
desalentar to discourage
desanimar to discourage
dimitir to resign, give up
rendirse to give up
renunciar to renounce, give up
tirar la toalla to throw in the towel

Ay...

similar terms

apuro *m* tight spot, embarrassment
aturdimiento *m* bewilderment, shock
bochorno *m* shame, embarrassment
confusión *f* confusion
desconcierto *m* bewilderment
escándalo *m* scandal
humillación *f* humiliation
incomodidad *f* discomfort
pena *f* embarrassment, discomfort
[most of L Am, except S Cone]
turbación *f* embarrassment, perturbation

aturdido(-a) bewildered, shocked
avergonzado(-a) embarrassed
confundido(-a) confused
desconcertado(-a) disconcerted, upset
incómodo(-a) awkward, uncomfortable
turbado(-a) embarrassed, upset

common expressions

Me pongo como un tomate.	I'm turning red as a beet (*lit.*, tomato).
Me siento avergonzado(-a).	I feel ashamed.
Me siento fatal.	I feel horrible.
Me siento tonto(-a).	I feel silly.
No sé dónde meterme.	I don't know what to do with myself (*lit.*, where to put myself).
¡Qué vergüenza!	How embarrassing!
Tengo pena.	I'm embarrassed. (*lit.*, I have discomfort. / I have sorrow.) [most of L Am]
¡Trágame, tierra!	Just kill me now! (*lit.*, Swallow me, earth!)
Traté de hacerme invisible.	I tried to make myself invisible.

abochornar to shame, embarrass
desconcertar to upset
no estar a gusto to be ill at ease
ruborizarse to blush
sonrojar(se) to blush
turbar to baffle, embarrass, unsettle

¡Huy!

similar terms

alarma *f* alarm
carne *f* **de gallina** goose bumps
escalofríos *mpl* shivers
espanto *m* fright, scare
pánico *m* panic
pavor *m* terror
temor *m* dread, fear
terror *m* terror, horror

ansioso(-a) anxious
aprensivo(-a) apprehensive
asustadizo(-a) easily frightened
miedoso(-a) fearful
preocupado(-a) worried
temeroso(-a) fearful
timorato(-a) God-fearing, fearful

common expressions

Doy diente con diente. My teeth are chattering.
◑ **Estoy cagado(-a).** I'm scared shitless. [S Cone, Spain]
Estoy muerto(-a) de miedo. I'm scared to death.
Me da escalofríos. It gives me the shivers.
Me dan ñáñaras. I get the willies. [Mex, parts of C Am]
Me pongo los pelos de punta. My hair is standing on end.
◑ **Tengo los cojones/huevos** I'm scared shitless. (*lit.*, I have my balls
  por corbata. as a necktie.)
Todavía estoy temblando. I'm still shaking.
Tuve un susto tremendo. I had a terrible scare.

◑ **no tener cojones** to not have balls
◑ **no tener huevos** to not have balls
rajarse to back down, chicken out
ser un gallina to be a chicken
sobresaltarse to jump, be startled
tener sudores fríos to break out in a cold sweat

asustón (asustona) *m/f* chicken, scaredy-cat [Mex]
◑ **cagado(-a)** *m/f* damn scaredy-cat [Spain]
◑ **cagón (cagona)** *m/f* damn scaredy-cat [S Cone, Spain]
◑ **cagueta** *m/f* damn scaredy-cat [Spain]
cobarde *m/f* coward
rajado(-a) *m/f* chicken, coward, wimp
rajón (rajona) *m/f* chicken, wimp

¡Gracias!

similar terms

agradecimiento *m* gratitude, thanks
reconocimiento *m* recognition, acknowledgment

common expressions

Estoy endeudado(-a) contigo.
I'm in your debt.

Hacerle bien al ingrato es lo mismo que ofenderlo. (REFRÁN)
Doing something nice for an ingrate is the same as offending him.

Me has sacado de un apuro.
You got me out of a jam.

Me quitaste las castañas del fuego.
You saved my bacon (*lit.*, pulled the chestnuts out of the fire for me).

Me salvaste el pellejo.
You saved my life (*lit.*, my hide/skin).

Mil gracias. Eres muy amable.
A thousand thanks. You're very kind.

No agradecen nada. Son unos desagradecidos/malagradecidos.
They aren't grateful for anything. They're ingrates.

No soy una persona desagradecida.
I'm not an ungrateful person.

No soy una persona malagradecida.
I'm not an ungrateful person.

Ser agradecidos es de bien nacidos. (REFRÁN)
It's important to recognize what people do for you. (*lit.*, Being grateful is the gift of well-born people.)

Te lo agradezco mucho.
I'm very thankful to you.

Te voy a pagar.
I'll pay you back.

agradecer to appreciate, be thankful
dar las gracias to thank
deberle a alguien to owe someone
estar endeudado(-a) con alguien to be indebted to someone
estar eternamente agradecido(-a) to be eternally grateful
estar profundamente agradecido(-a) to be deeply grateful

similar terms

bienstar *m* well-being
buena condición *f* **física** good physical condition

common expressions

Como demasiado.	I eat too much.
Después de dejar de fumar, me siento rebosante de salud.	Since I quit smoking, I feel very healthy (*lit.*, brimming with health).
Es por falta de ejercicio.	It's due to lack of exercise.
Es sana como una manzana.	She's fit as a fiddle (*lit.*, healthy as an apple).
Estoy a dieta.	I'm on a diet.
Estoy barrigón (barrigona).	I've got a bit of a paunch.
Estoy en una forma increíble.	I'm in incredible shape.
Estoy en una forma magnífica.	I'm in magnificent shape.
Guarda la línea.	She keeps her figure.
Sigo un régimen.	I'm on a diet.
Tiene una cintura de avispa.	She has a narrow (*lit.*, wasp's) waist.
Tiene una silueta muy bonita.	She has a nice figure.

aumentar de peso to gain weight
bajar de peso to lose weight
comer frutas y verduras to eat fruits and vegetables
dejar de fumar to stop smoking
estar de buena salud to be in good health
estar de mala salud to be in poor health
estar en muy buena forma física to be in great shape
estar lleno(-a) de energía to be full of energy
hacer deportes to play sports
hacer ejercicios (aeróbicos) to work out, do (aerobic) exercises
ir al gimnasio to go to the gym

similar terms

disimulo *m* deception
doblez *f* duplicity
duplicidad *f* duplicity
engaño *m* deceit
falsedad *f* falseness
mentira *f* **por omisión** lie by omission

adulador(a) flattering, sycophantic; *m/f* flatterer
desleal disloyal
falso(-a) fake
furtivo(-a) furtive
mentiroso(-a) lying; *m/f* liar
solapado(-a) sneaky
traidor(a) treacherous; *m/f* traitor

common expressions

Cara de Viernes Santo y hechos de Carnaval. (REFRÁN)
His look says Good Friday but his actions say Mardi Gras.

Con su pinta de santurrón, se gana la comunión sin la confesión.
With his goody-goody looks, you could give him communion without confession.

Cuídate, que es de los que apuñalean por la espalda.
Be careful, he's a backstabber.

Es un Judas. Es más falso que Judas Iscariote.
He's a Judas. He's falser than Judas Iscariot.

actuar con disimulo to hide one's true thoughts or intentions
cambiar de camisa to change sides, be a turncoat (*lit.*, change shirt)
cambiar de chaqueta to change sides, be a turncoat (*lit.*, change jacket)
comer a dos carrillos to do what's most convenient, serve two (or more) masters (*lit.*, eat with two cheeks)
dar gato por liebre to pass something off that is inferior (*lit.*, to give cat for rabbit)
disimular to hide one's true thoughts or intentions
hacer algo por debajo de cuerda to do something dishonestly (*lit.*, under rope)
hacerse el inocente to play the innocent
llorar lágrimas de cocodrilo to cry crocodile tears
tener dos caras to be two-faced
tirar la piedra y esconder la mano to do something and cover it up (*lit.*, to throw the stone and hide one's hand)
traicionar to betray, double-cross

diablo *m* **vendiendo cruces** hypocrite (*lit.*, the devil selling crosses)
◯ **lameculos** *m* brownnoser, ass kisser
mosquita *f* **muerta** hypocrite, someone who pretends to be innocent but takes advantage of others (*lit.*, a dead fly)

¡Eureka!

similar terms

asociación *f* **de ideas** association of ideas
concepto *m* concept
conciencia *f* awareness
descubrimiento *m* discovery
genio *m* genius
hallazgo *m* finding, discovery
iluminación *f* illumination
imaginación *f* imagination
invento *m* invention
noción *f* notion

astuto(-a) clever
brillante brilliant
creativo(-a) creative
imaginativo(-a) imaginative
inteligente intelligent
inventivo(-a) inventive

common expressions

¿Cuál fue tu fuente de inspiración? What was the source of your inspiration?
Es una obra maestra. It's a work of art.
La idea me vino de súbito. The idea suddenly came to me.
La imaginación es el laboratorio en donde se fabrica todo a nuestro gusto. (REFRÁN) Imagination is the laboratory in which everything is custom-made.
"¡Quítame, oh Dios, el oro y la fortuna, pero vuélveme a dar las ilusiones!" (Ramón de Campoamor) "Take from me, God, gold and fortune, but give me back my illusions!"

crear to create
devanarse los sesos to rack one's brains
encontrar la solución to find the solution
fomentar la cultura to foster culture
ganar un premio (el premio Nóbel) to win a prize (the Nobel Prize)
inventar to invent
ser más listo(-a) que el hambre to be sharp as a tack (*lit.*, sharper than hunger)
tener una idea to have an idea

corriente *f* **de pensamiento** intellectual trend, school of thought
musa *f* muse

similar terms

amargura *f* bitterness
competencia *f* competition
decepción *f* disappointment
desconfianza *f* distrust
deseo *m* desire
envidia *f* envy
odio *m* hatred
rivalidad *f* rivalry
sospecho *m* suspicion
vigilancia *f* surveillance

celoso(-a) jealous
envidioso(-a) de los bienes de otros
    envious of other people's property
muerto(-a) de envidia dying of envy

common expressions

Donde hay celos, hay amor.
(REFRÁN)
Esto huele mal.
Gato escaldado, del agua fría
huye. (REFRÁN)
Hombre, te estoy vigilando.
Marido celoso no tiene reposo.
(REFRÁN)
Me puso una mosca detrás de
las orejas.

Where there's love, there's jealousy.

I smell a rat. (*lit.*, This smells bad.)
Once bitten, twice shy. (*lit.*, A scalded
    cat flees from cold water.)
Dude, I've got my eye on you.
The jealous husband has no rest.

That set me thinking. (*lit.*, That put
    a fly behind my ears.)

codiciar to covet
desconfiar to distrust
dudar to doubt
envidiar to envy
estar a la defensiva to be on one's guard, be on the defensive
palidecer de envidia to be green (*lit.*, pale) with envy
presentir to have a premonition, inkling
ser suspicaz to be suspicious
sospechar to suspect
tener celos de alguien to be jealous of someone
tener ganas de to want, desire

¡Yupi!

similar terms

alborozo *m* bliss
alegría *f* happiness
delirio *m* delirium
euforia *f* euphoria
explosión *f* **de júbilo** outburst of joy
exultación *f* exaltation
felicidad *f* happiness
regocijo *m* joy, delight

common expressions

Da saltos de alegría.	He's jumping for joy.
Está de muy bien humor.	He's in a very good mood.
Está en la gloria.	She's in seventh heaven.
Está encantada de la vida.	She's happy as can be.
Está rebosante de alegría.	She's brimming with happiness.
Está requetecontenta.	She's super-happy.
Estalla de júbilo.	She's bursting with joy.
¡Hurra!	Hooray!
La vida le sonríe.	Life is great for him (*lit.*, smiling at him).
Se siente fantástica.	She feels fantastic.
¡Yupi!	Yippee!

¡Je je!

similar terms

carcajadas *fpl* roaring (loud) laughter
hilaridad *f* hilarity
risotadas *fpl* guffaws

common expressions

¡Es chistosísimo(-a)!	It's very funny!
¡Es desternillante!	It's side-splitting!
¡Es divertidísimo(-a)!	It's really entertaining!
¡Estoy muerto(-a) de risa!	I'm dying of laughter!
○ ¡Me meo de la risa.	I'm laughing so hard, I'm peeing!
Me reventé de la risa.	I cracked up laughing.
"No se olviden nunca de reír. Porque para sufrir siempre habrá mucho tiempo." (Mario Moreno (Cantinflas))	"Never forget to laugh. Because there will always be lots of time to suffer."
¡Voy a morirme de la risa!	I'm going to die laughing!
Ya basta, ¡estoy doblado(-a) de risa!	Stop, I'm doubled over with laughter!

bromear to joke
○ **cagarse de la risa** to wet oneself laughing (*colloq.*) [L Am]
carcajear to laugh heartily
contar chistes to tell jokes
○ **descojonarse de la risa** to wet oneself laughing (*colloq.*) [Spain]
desternillarse de risa to split one's sides laughing
doblarse de risa to double up with laughter
echarse a reír to burst out laughing
gastar bromas to banter
llorarse de risa to laugh till one cries
partirse de risa to burst out laughing, crack up
reírse a carcajadas to guffaw, laugh heartily
reírse a lo loco to laugh like a fool
reírse a mandíbula batiente to roar with laughter
reírse ahogadamente to chortle, chuckle
reventar de la risa to burst out laughing, crack up
torcerse de risa to double up with laughter
troncharse de risa to crack up with laughter [Spain]

similar terms

agrado *m* pleasure, liking
felicidad *f* happiness
placer *m* pleasure
serenidad *f* serenity

contento(-a) glad, pleased
encantado(-a) delighted
satisfecho(-a) satisfied
sereno(-a) serene

common expressions

Es la satisfacción de un trabajo bien hecho.	It's the satisfaction of a job well done.
¡Es perfecto!	It's perfect!
Espero que se resuelva el asunto a su entera satisfacción.	I hope the issue will be resolved to your complete satisfaction.
Estoy en paz, contento(-a).	I'm at peace, content.
Fue un enorme satisfacción poder conocerlo.	It was an enormous pleasure to be able to meet him.
Me siento bien.	I feel good.
Misión cumplida.	Mission accomplished.
No me falta nada.	I have everything I need. (*lit.*, Nothing is lacking to me.)
Ojalá sea de su agrado.	I hope it's to your liking.
Tuve la satisfacción de hablarles.	I had the satisfaction of speaking to them.

¡Zzz!

similar terms

adormecimiento *m* drowsiness, falling asleep
agotamiento *m* exhaustion
cansancio *m* tiredness
fatiga *f* fatigue
insomnio *m* insomnia
modorra *f* drowsiness
reposo *m* rest
siesta *f* nap
somnolencia *f* drowsiness
sopor *m* sleepiness

common expressions

No pegué los ojos en toda la noche.	I didn't close (*lit.*, glue shut) my eyes all night.
No puedo mantenerme con los ojos abiertos.	I can't keep my eyes open.
Pasé la noche en blanco/vela.	I was awake all night. (*lit.*, I spent the night on blank/watch.)
Soy insomne; me cuesta mucho dormir.	I'm an insomniac; it's hard for me to sleep.
Tengo sueño.	I'm sleepy.
Voy a meterme en el sobre.	I'm going to put myself to bed (*lit.*, in my envelope). [Ec, S Cone, Spain]

conciliar el sueño to get to sleep, be able to sleep
desvelar to keep awake, stay up
dormir a cuerpo de rey to sleep like a king
dormir a pierna suelta to sleep soundly (*lit.*, with loose leg)
dormir como un lirón to sleep like a log (*lit.*, like a dormouse)
dormir como un tronco to sleep like a log
dormirse parado(-a) to fall asleep on one's feet
echar una siesta to take a nap
estar medio dormido(-a) to be half asleep
luchar contra el sueño to fight off sleep
pasar una noche toledana to have a sleepless night (*lit.*, a Toledo night) [Spain]
planchar la oreja to sleep, lie down (*lit.*, to iron one's ear)
roncar to snore
sobar to snooze [Spain]

despertador *m* alarm clock
dormilón (dormilona) *m/f* sleepyhead, late riser, someone who sleeps a lot
madrugador(a) *m/f* early riser
sueño *m* **profundo** deep sleep
terapia *f* **de sueño** sleep therapy
trasnochador(a) *m/f* night owl

¡Ay!

similar terms

aflicción *f* affliction
angustia *f* anguish
dolor *m* **agudo** sharp pain
dolor *m* **atroz** terrible pain
pena *f* sorrow
tormento *m* torment

common expressions

¡Ay! ¡Me duele mucho!	Ouch! It hurts a lot!
Entré bizco(-a) y salí cojo(-a).	It went from bad to worse. (*lit.*, I came in cross-eyed and left limping.)
Es como parir chayotes.	It's impossible (*lit.*, like giving birth to chayotes (a prickly vegetable)). [Mex]
Es intolerable.	I can't take it. (*lit.*, It's intolerable.)
Es un suplicio.	It's pure torture.
Es una tortura.	It's pure torture.
Estoy contigo.	I feel for you. (*lit.*, I am with you.)
Las grandes penas se llevan por dentro.	The greatest suffering is done in silence. (*lit.*, The greatest sorrows are carried on the inside.)
Lo estoy pasando negras.	I'm having a heck of a time. [Mex, S Cone, Spain]
○ **Lo estoy pasando putas.**	I'm having a hell of a time. [Mex, S Cone, Spain]
Me parte el alma verte sufrir así.	It breaks my heart (*lit.*, splits my soul) to see you suffer like this.
Para colmo de desgracias...	On top of everything else ... (*lit.*, For the height of misfortunes ...)
Te acompaño en el dolor.	I feel for you. (*lit.*, I accompany you in your pain.)

acompañar a alguien en el dolor to feel for someone in his/her sorrow
pasar por un auténtico calvario to go through a real ordeal
retorcerse de dolor to writhe in agony
sufrir el martirio to suffer agony (*lit.*, martyrdom)
sufrir un auténtico calvario to go through a real ordeal

¿Cómo?

similar terms

asombro *m* astonishment
aturdimiento *m* bewilderment, confusion
estupor *m* amazement
incredulidad *f* disbelief
negación *f* denial
perplejidad *f* bewilderment

asombrado(-a) astonished
atónito(-a) aghast
boquiabierto(-a) flabbergasted
    (*lit.*, openmouthed)
escéptico(-a) skeptical
estupefacto(-a) awestruck
incrédulo(-a) incredulous
sorprendido(-a) surprised

common expressions

¡Caramba!	Wow! / Jeez!
¡Caray!	Wow! / Jeez!
¡Cayó como bomba!	It was like a bombshell!
Dime que estoy soñando.	Tell me I'm dreaming.
¡Dios mío! ¡Dios santo!	My goodness! Good Lord!
Es insólito (pero cierto).	It's unheard of (but true).
Fue imprevisto.	It was unforeseen.
Fue inesperado.	It was unexpected.
¿Hablas en serio?	Are you serious?
¡Híjole!	Wow! / Jeez! [Mex]
¡La pucha!	Wow! / Jeez! [L Am]
Me alucinó la noticia.	The news stunned me. [Spain]
Me dejó frío(-a).	I was stunned. (*lit.*, It left me cold.)
Me dejó helado(-a).	I was stunned. (*lit.*, It left me frozen.)
¡Ostras!	Holy cow! (*lit.*, Oysters!) [Spain]
¡Pucha!	Wow! / Jeez! [L Am]
¡Qué barbaridad!	How awful!
¡Qué bárbaro!	How awful!
¡Será una broma!	It must be a joke!
Si no lo veo, no lo creo.	I don't believe my eyes. (*lit.*, If I weren't seeing it, I wouldn't believe it.)

caer de las nubes to come out of the blue (*lit.*, fall out of the clouds)
dudar to doubt
negar to deny
quedarse pasmado(-a) to be dumbfounded

similar terms

descontento *m* dissatisfaction
exasperación *f* exasperation
insatisfacción *f* dissatisfaction
irritabilidad *f* irritability
sensibilidad *f* sensitivity

delicado(-a) fussy, sensitive
emotivo(-a) emotional
hipersensible hypersensitive
impresionable impressionable
irascible touchy, irritable
picajón (picajona) touchy, easily offended
picajoso(-a) touchy, easily offended
puntilloso(-a) fussy, punctilious
quisquilloso(-a) sensitive, fussy, touchy
sensible sensitive
susceptible touchy; susceptible

common expressions

Es un fosforito.	He has a short fuse (*lit.*, is a little match). [parts of L Am]
¿Qué bicho te está picando?	What's bugging you? (*lit.*, What bug is biting you?)
¿Qué mosca te está picando?	What's bugging you? (*lit.*, What fly is biting you?)
Se alteró.	He had a change in mood.
Se enoja por cualquier cosita.	She gets angry about every little thing.
Tiene una sensibilidad a flor de piel.	His sensitivity is obvious (*lit.*, at the flower of the skin).
Todo lo fastidia.	Everything bothers him.
Todo lo molesta.	Everything bothers him.
Todo lo saca de las casillas.	Everything rattles his cage (*lit.*, takes him out of his little boxes).
Todo lo saca de onda.	Everything bugs him (*lit.*, takes him out of sound wave). [L Am]
Toma las cosas a pecho.	She takes things very seriously (*lit.*, to chest).

¿Qué hacer?

similar terms

dilema *m* dilemma
duda *f* doubt
indecisión *f* indecision
inquietud *f* worry
inseguridad *f* insecurity
irresolución *f* lack of resolution
perplejidad *f* puzzlement, confusion
preocupación *f* worry
principio *m* **de Heisenberg** Heisenberg's
  uncertainty principle
vacilación *f* hesitation

desorientado(-a) disoriented
incierto(-a) unsure
inconstante changing, inconstant
indeciso(-a) indecisive
indeterminado(-a) uncertain
inseguro(-a) unsure
vacilante hesitating

common expressions

Avanzamos a tientas en la oscuridad...	We're feeling our way in the dark ...
El futuro es inseguro.	The future is uncertain.
Estamos en ascuas.	We're on pins and needles (*lit.*, on embers).
Estamos entre dos aguas.	We're on the fence (*lit.*, between two waters).
Estamos titubeando.	We're waffling.
Estamos totalmente despistados.	We're completely off course.
No sabemos a qué carta quedarnos.	We don't know which way to turn (*lit.*, which card to keep).
Nos perdemos en conjeturas.	We're just making things up.
Por si acaso.	Just in case.
Por si las moscas.	Just in case. (*lit.*, In case the flies.) (*colloq.*)
Sabe Dios.	God knows.
Si Dios quiere.	God willing.
Ya no estamos seguros de nada.	We're not sure of anything.

¡Milagro!

similar terms

admiración *f* admiration
emoción *f* excitement
encanto *m* enchantment
entusiasmo *m* enthusiasm
éxtasis *m* ecstasy

arrebatado(-a) (de) carried away (with)
arrobado(-a) (de) carried away (with)
asombrado(-a) astonished, amazed
boquiabierto(-a) flabbergasted
  (*lit.*, openmouthed)
embelesado(-a) fascinated
entusiasmado(-a) enthusiastic
estupefacto(-a) awestruck
fascinado(-a) fascinated
hechizado(-a) bewitched
incrédulo(-a) incredulous
sorprendido(-a) surprised

common expressions

¡Es el despelote!	It's the best! [Spain]
¡Es estupendo(-a)!	It's great!
¡Es la octava maravilla!	It's fantastic (*lit.*, the eighth wonder)!
¡Es una obra maestra!	It's a marvel (*lit.*, master work)!
¡Extraordinario(-a)! ¡Fantástico(-a)!	Extraordinary! Fantastic!
¡Me dejó con los ojos como platos!	It left me with my eyes as big as saucers (*lit.*, plates)!
¡Me quedé boquiabierto(-a)!	I was flabbergasted (*lit.*, openmouthed)!
¡Milagro!	It's a miracle!
¡Qué belleza!	What beauty! / How beautiful!
¡Qué maravilla!	How wonderful!
¡Todo funciona a las mil maravillas!	Everything's working wonderfully (*lit.*, to a thousand marvels)!
¡Todo va a las mil maravillas!	Everything's going wonderfully (*lit.*, to a thousand marvels)!

Let's see how you did on the Humorómetro (pages 92–94) and what it reveals about how emotional you are.

20–30 You're a pretty emotional person, capable of losing your cool easily, fretting about things, even going off the deep end. It might be good to lighten up a bit.

31–39 You're pretty even-tempered. You tend to take things calmly and don't get too full of yourself.

40–50 You're calm and collected, not given to frights or fits. A good person to have in a pinch, but maybe you'd like to spice up your life just a bit.

appearance and gestures

facial descriptions

hair 120
the face 125
facial types 126
the body in slang 129
how do I look? 130

la agencia de contactos 132

body language

confrontation 134
interjections 136
gestures
food and drink 140
insults 141
praise, promises, annoyance 142
the senses 143
talk 144
time and money 145
transportation 146
miscellaneous 147

afro
Afro

cola de caballo
ponytail

colita
rattail

colitas
pigtails

corte cepillo
flattop, brush cut

corte de pelo militar
military cut

related expressions

cabellera *f* hair, head of hair
cuero *m* **cabelludo** scalp
mechón *f* **de pelo** lock, strand of hair
pelos *mpl* hairs
raíz *f* root

• • •

tipo *m* **de pelo** type of hair

el pelo ____ ____ hair
  brillante shiny
  chino curly [Mex, parts of C Am]
  corto short
  crespo curly
  encrespado curly

engominado slicked-back, gelled
fino fine
grasoso greasy
lacio limp, straight
largo long
liso straight
lustroso shiny
ondulado wavy
quebradizo brittle
reseco very dry
rizado curly
seco dry
sedoso silky
suave soft

• • •

corte hongo [L Am]
mushroom cut, bowl cut, dutch boy

cresta de gallo, "punk"
mohawk, punk

engominado
slicked back, gelled

flequillo
bangs

esponjado [Mex, C Am]
bouffant, beehive

hippie
hippie

---

color *m* **del pelo** hair color

el pelo _____ _____ hair
  blanco y negro salt-and-pepper
  café claro light brown
  café oscuro dark brown
  canoso graying
  castaño chestnut
  gris gray
  negro black
  negro azabache jet-black
  plateado silvery
  rojizo auburn, reddish
  rubio blond
  teñido dyed

pelirrojo(-a) *m/f* red-haired person, redhead
primera cana *f* first gray hair

•••

volumen *m* **del pelo**
  hair thickness

el pelo _____ _____ hair
  abundante lots of
  grueso thick
  ralo thin

calvicie *f* baldness
calvo(-a) *m/f* chrome-dome; *adj* bald

peinado hacia atrás
off the face, combed back

moño
bun

pelo corto
short

pelo muy crespo
frizzy

pelo parado
spiked hair

implante *m* **de pelo**
  hair transplant
melena *f* mane
remolino *m* cowlick
tupé *f* hairpiece, toupee
perder el pelo to lose one's hair
quedarse calvo(-a) to go bald

•••

el pelo desordenado
  hair in a mess

el pelo ____ ____ hair
  alborotado tousled
  desgreñado messy
  desmelenado ruffled
  despeinado uncombed
  despelucado unkempt (*colloq.*)
  enredado tangled

greñudo long and sloppy
  [Mex, C Am, Col]
indomable wild

•••

accesorios *mpl* accessories
brillantina *f* hair cream
diadema *m* headband
extensiones *fpl* extensions
ganchita *f* pin
gancho *m* barrette
gomina *f* gel
horquilla *f* pin
laca *f* hairspray
lazo *m* ribbon, bow
pasador *m* **de pelo** barrette
peine *m* comb
peluca *f* wig

rapado
shaved

rastas (trenzas estilo jamaiquino)
dreadlocks
(Jamaican-style braids)

raya en medio
parted in the middle

rizado
curly

raya al lado
parted on the side

permanente *m* perm(anent)
pinza *f* clip
plancha *f* **de pelo** hair straightener
postizo *m* hairpiece, toupee, wig
red *f* hairnet
redecilla *f* hairnet
rulo *m* hair curler/roller
secador *m* **de pelo** hair dryer
tenazas *fpl* **de rizar** curling iron
tinte *m* dye

• • •

cepillado *m* brushing
corte *m* **de pelo** haircut
cuidado *m* **del pelo** hair care
estilista *m/f* hair stylist
peinado *m* hairdo, hairstyle
peluquería *f* barber shop, beauty salon

salón *m* **de belleza**
hair salon

aclarar to lighten
alisar to straighten
arreglar el pelo to fix one's hair
cepillarse to brush one's hair
cortar (las puntas) to cut (the ends)
decolorar to bleach
desenredar to untangle
entresacar to thin (out)
lavarse la cabeza to wash one's hair (*lit.*, head)
peinarse to comb/brush one's hair
rapar to shave off, shear
recortar to trim
rizar to curl
teñir to dye

trenzas
braids

**roquero,
estilo "Elvis"**
rocker, Elvis cut

trenzitas
cornrows

• • •

modismos *mpl* hair idioms

Nunca falta un pelo en la sopa. There's always a hitch/problem (*lit.*, hair in the soup).

jalarse los pelos to pull your hair out (with anger)

no tener pelos en la lengua to talk clearly, without mincing words (*lit.*, to not have hair on the tongue)

poner a alguien los pelos de punta to make someone's hair stand on end, give someone the creeps (from fear)

salvarse por un pelo to be saved by the bell (*lit.*, by a hair)

tomarle el pelo a alguien to pull someone's leg (*lit.*, hair), tease

con pelos y señales in great detail (*lit.*, with hairs and gestures)

cuando la rana eche pelos when hell freezes over (*lit.*, when the frog sprouts hair) [L Am]

por un pelo by a little bit (*lit.*, by a hair)

hombre *m* **de pelo en pecho** real he-man (*lit.*, man with hair on his chest)

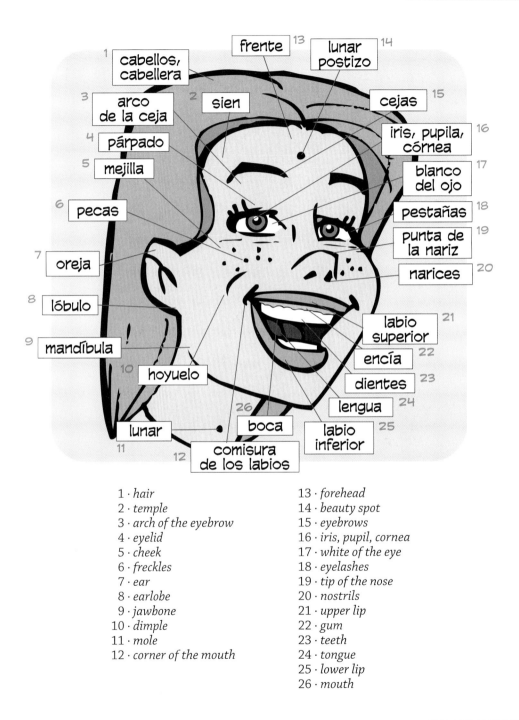

1 · hair
2 · temple
3 · arch of the eyebrow
4 · eyelid
5 · cheek
6 · freckles
7 · ear
8 · earlobe
9 · jawbone
10 · dimple
11 · mole
12 · corner of the mouth
13 · forehead
14 · beauty spot
15 · eyebrows
16 · iris, pupil, cornea
17 · white of the eye
18 · eyelashes
19 · tip of the nose
20 · nostrils
21 · upper lip
22 · gum
23 · teeth
24 · tongue
25 · lower lip
26 · mouth

angular, de facciones pronunciadas
angular, craggy

alargada, cara de hacha
elongated, hatchet face

arrugada, llena de baches
wrinkled, rutted

cara de caballo
horsy

con mejillas sobresalientes
with high cheekbones

con barbilla prominente
with a prominent chin

devastada, hinchada, cara de cansado
ravaged, swollen, tired-looking

con rasgos finos y armoniosos
with fine and harmonious features

hinchada, gorda, regordeta
puffy (swollen), fat, chubby

huesuda, delgada, demacrada
bony, thin, emaciated

irregular, torcida
irregular, crooked

ovalada
oval

redonda
round

rechoncha
chubby

related expressions

arrugas *fpl* wrinkles
color *m* **natural** natural color
estructura *f* **facial** facial structure
rasgos *mpl* features
tez *f* complexion
tono *m* **de piel** skin tone

•••

la cara ____ ____ face
  arrugada wrinkled
  bronceada tanned
  cenicienta ashen
  cubierta de granos pimply
  descolorida faded
  devastada ravaged
  manchada blotchy
  pálida pale

quemada por el sol sunburned
radiante bright
seca dry

•••

la cara ____ ____ face
  cansada tired
  demacrada haggard
  fruncida frowning
  hermética poker
  hosca sullen
  relajada relaxed
  seria serious
  severa stern
  sonriente smiling
  tranquila calm

•••

cuidado *m* **del cutis** facial care

lifting *m* face-lift

maquillaje *m* makeup

rejuvenecimiento *m* **de la cara**
facial rejuvenation

• • •

related terms

actitud *f* attitude

aire *m* look, air

apariencia *f* appearance

aspecto *m* look, aspect

aspecto *m* **exterior** outward
appearance

carácter *m* character

estatura *f* stature, height

estilo *m* style

gesto *m* facial expression

imagen *f* image

"look" *m* look

perfil *m* profile

personalidad *f* personality

pinta *f* look, appearance (*colloq.*)

porte *m* bearing

silueta *f* silhouette

These needles are the pits. Are they for learning a foreign language or for some acupuncture session?

As long as they don't put any weight on me, they're fine!

verse bien to look good

Ella se ve saludable y en forma. Sus mejillas son rojas como las rosas, gracias al tiempo que pasó en la playa. Su cara es reluciente. Está sana como una manzana.

She looks healthy and fit. Her cheeks are red as roses, thanks to the time she spent on the beach. Her face is beaming. She's fit as a fiddle (*lit.*, healthy as an apple).

verse fatal to look terrible

A este tipo se le ve como un muerto recalentado. Sus rasgos son alargados, y parece cansado y pálido. Se le ve como si tuviera resaca. Está por los suelos. Su piel es amarillenta, y tiene un aspecto fantasmal.

This guy looks like death warmed over. His features are stretched, and he looks beat and pale. He looks like he's got a hangover. He's down in the dumps. His skin is sallow, and he has a ghostly appearance.

rebosante de salud brimming with health

Este hombre está verdaderamente en forma. Se le ve rebosante de salud. Es un tipo radiante, feliz, abierto de mente y atractivo.

This man is truly in shape. He's brimming with health. This guy beams; he looks happy, open, and attractive.

rígida uptight

Esta mujer parece que se ha tragado un palo de escoba. Su boca está fruncida como el culo de una gallina. Se le ve tensa y nerviosa.
This woman looks like she's swallowed a broomstick. Her mouth is as tight as a chicken's butt hole. She looks tense and nervous.

ecuánime easygoing

Las personas como este tipo son de buen carácter por naturaleza: tranquilos y de mente abierta. Toman las cosas con calma. Se ven relajados y contentos.
People like this guy are good-natured: calm and open-minded. They take life as it comes. They look relaxed and content.

con ojeras with bags under the eyes

Este tipo tiene unas ojeras enormes. Parece agotado, rendido. Es un zombi.
This guy has enormous bags under his eyes. He looks worn out, beat. He's a zombie.

You run an online dating service, but you're threatened by a class-action lawsuit over false advertising! To ensure the accuracy of the information on your Web site, write new descriptions for your clients, based on these photos from their applications.

1. _____   2. _____   3. _____

_____   _____   _____

_____   _____   _____

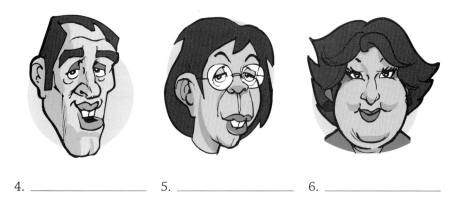

4. _____   5. _____   6. _____

_____   _____   _____

_____   _____   _____

7. _____

_____

_____

8. _____

_____

_____

9. _____

_____

_____

10. _____

_____

_____

11. _____

_____

_____

12. _____

_____

_____

el pleito • the quarrel

You're always looking for trouble, picking fights.

Siempre andas buscando problemas, provocando broncas.

¡Qué buscapleitos eres!

Eres mezquino, tacaño, presumido y grosero.

What a troublemaker you are!

You always contradict everyone.

Siempre llevas la contraria.

You're mean, stingy, stuck-up, and rude.

No se puede contigo.

You're impossible.

Don't screw with me!

If you're looking for trouble, here I am! (lit., He who looks, finds!)

¡El que busca, encuentra!

¡No jodas!

¡Vamos a terminar dándonos!

We're going to end up at blows with each other!

related terms

agresivo(-a) aggressive
belicoso(-a) bellicose, given to fighting
brutal brutal, violent
combativo(-a) combative

pendenciero(-a) quarrelsome, given to fighting
respondón (respondona) sassy, answering back
violento(-a) violent

altercado *m* altercation, quarrel
bochinche *m* brawl, noisy fight
  [most of L Am, not Mex]
bronca *f* brawl, dispute
conflicto *m* conflict
culpa *f* blame
discusión *f* argument

disputa *f* argument
insulto *m* insult
jaleo *m* uproar, brawl
pelea *f* fight
pleito *m* argument, fight
riña *f* squabble
ruptura *f* breakup

Armaron un escándalo.	They made a big scene.
Esto va a terminar mal.	This is going to end badly.
Hubo una de todos los diablos.	There was a devil of a fight.
La reunión se degeneró.	The meeting got out of hand.
Les gusta hacer teatro.	They like to make a scene.
Les plantaron cara.	They stood up to them.
Montaron un numerito.	They raised a fuss.
Se armó la gorda.	All hell broke loose.

el aumento • the raise

Mírame la cara ahora.
Tengo las cejas levantadas
y fruncidas.
No sonrío.
Se me ha nublado la mirada
severamente.
Mis mejillas se contraen
y se expanden.
Mis dientes rechinan.
Siento que echo humo
por la nariz.
Una mueca de disgusto
se refleja en mi cara.
Me estoy mordiendo los labios,
mi cara tiembla nerviosamente
y los músculos y las venas
de mi cuello están a punto
de reventar.
Mis ojos están a punto
de salirse de sus órbitas.
Me estoy poniendo morado
de la ira.
¿Son estas señales de
impaciencia o simplemente
sentimientos de rabia
acumulada?

Look at my face now.
I'm raising my eyebrows
and frowning.
I'm not smiling.
My look has clouded over
severely.
My cheeks are expanding
and contracting.
My teeth are grinding.
I feel like smoke is coming
out my nose.
A grimace of disgust
is reflected on my face.
I'm biting my lips, my face
is trembling nervously,
and the muscles and veins
of my neck are about to burst.
My eyes are about to pop
out of their sockets.
I'm turning purple
with anger.
Are these signs of impatience
or just accumulated rage?

Bueno, este...
¿qué tal si hablamos
sobre el aumento de
sueldo en algunos años...
cuando se sienta
mejor?

Um . . . how about
if we talk about my
raise in a couple
of years—when
you're feeling better?

¡A comer!	Dinnertime!
¡A dormir!	Go to sleep!
¡A la mierda!	Go to hell! The hell with it!
¡A la puta!	Go to hell! The hell with it!
¡A que no te atreves!	Bet you don't dare!
¡Abajo...!	Down with ...!
¡Adiós!	Bye!
¡Aguas!	Look out! [Mex, C Am]
¡Ajá!	Uh-huh!
¡Alto!	Stop! Halt!
¡Amén!	Amen!
¡Anda!	Wow! [Spain]
¡Ándale!	Right! That's it! [Mex]
¡Ánimo!	Hang in there!
¡Arre, arre!	Giddyup!
¡Arriba...!	Hooray for ...!
¡Así es!	You bet! That's it!
¡Así se hace!	Way to go!
¡Aupa!	Go! (sports) [Spain]
¡Auxilio!	Help!
¡Ave María!	Good heavens!
¡Ay!	Ouch!
¡Bah!	Harrumph! Bah!

¡Basta (ya)!	Enough (already)!
¡Bien hecho!	Good for you! Well done!
¡Bis!	Encore!
¡Bla, bla, bla!	Blah, blah, blah!
¡Buaaa!	Boo hoo!
¡Buena lección!	That'll teach you!
¡Cállate!	Shut up!
¡Caramba!	Wow! Holy smoke!
¡Caray!	Darn! Wow!
¡Casi!	Almost!
¡Cataplum!	Boom!
¡Chau!	Bye-bye! [S Cone]
¡Chau-chau!	Bye-bye! [S Cone]
¡Chíngale!	Fuck it! [Mex]
¡Chócala!	Put it here (for a handshake)!
¡Cierra la boca!	Shut up!
¡Cierto!	Sure thing! Right!
¡Claro!	Sure!
¡Cojones!	Damn! [Cuba, Spain]
¡Cómo!	What!
¡Cómo no!	Of course!
¡Con permiso!	Excuse me (for something I'm about to do)!
¡Coño!	Damn! [Mex, Carib, Spain]

¡Correcto! — Right!
¡Cuidado! — Be careful!
¡Dame cinco (dedos)! — Give me five!
¡De acuerdo! — Okay then! Agreed!
¡De ninguna manera! — No way!
¡Diablos! — Holy cow! [Mex, Carib]
¡Dios mío! — Good Lord!
¡Dios santo! — Good Lord!
¡Eh! — Hey!
¡Epa, epa! — Hey! [Carib]
¡Es lo máximo! — It's the best!
¡Eso! — Bingo! That's it!
¡Eso es! — That's it!
¡Espérate! — Wait a minute!
¡Esto está de la jodida! — This sucks!
¡Estupendo! — Great!
¡Eureka! — Eureka!
¡Exacto! — Exactly!
¡Fenomenal! — Fantastic! Great!
¡Fondo blanco! — Bottoms up!
¡Fúchila! — Yuck! Ewww! [Mex, C Am]
¡Fuego! — Fire!
¡Fuera! — Get out!
¡Gracias! — Thanks!

¡Gratis! — Free!
¡Hasta la vista! — See you!
¡Hasta pronto! — See you soon!
¡Híjole! — Jeez! Wow! [Mex, C Am]
¡Hola! — Hello! Hi!
¡Hombre! — Man! Dude! (to man or woman)
¡Hostia(s)! — God damn it! [Spain]
¡Huácala! — Yuck! Ewww! [Mex, C Am, parts of Carib]
¡Hurra! — Hooray!
¡Inútil! — Useless!
¡Ja! — Ha!
¡Ja, ja!/¡Je, je! — Ha ha!
¡Joer! — Damn! [Spain]
¡Lástima! — Too bad!
¡Levántate! — Stand up!
¡Magnífico! — Great!
¡Mala suerte! — Tough luck!
¡Me cago en Dios! — Fuck it! [Spain]
¡Miércoles! — Shoot!
¡Mierda! — Shit! Crap!
¡Mmmm! — Hmmm! Yum!
¡Momento! — Just a minute!
¡Muévete! — Move it! Get going!

¡Naranjas!	Nope!
¡Ni a palos!	No way!
¡Ni cagando!	No damn way!
¡Ni hablar!	No way! Don't even mention it!
¡Ni loco(-a)!	No way!
¡Ni mierda!	No damn way!
¡Ni soñar!	Not even in your dreams! Dream on!
¡Nones para los botones/ preguntones!	No! None! None for you!
¡O!	Oh!
¡Oiga!	Hey, you!
¡Ojo!	Look out!
¡Olé!	Olé!
¡Olvídalo!	Forget about it!
¡Órale!	All right! Okay! [Mex, C Am]
¡Ostras!	Darn! [Spain]
¡Oye!	Hey, you!
¡Paf!	Pow!
¡Pan!	Bang!
¡Pan! ¡Pan!	Bang! Bang!
¡Para nada!	No way!
¡Párate!	Stop!
¡Perdón!	Sorry!
¡Permiso!	Passing through!

¡Píntate!	Beat it! [Mex]
¡Plas!	Splash!
¡Pobrecito(-a)!	Poor thing!
¡Ponte a pie!	Stand up!
¡Ponte las pilas!	Snap to it! Get a move on!
¡Por favor!	Oh, please!
¡Por supuesto!	Of course!
¡Puah!	Yuck! Ewww! [Spain]
¡Pucha!/ ¡La pucha!	Darn! [L Am]
¡Pum!	Boom!
¡Pum! ¡Pum!	Bang! Bang!
¡Puta!	Damn!
¡Puta madre!	Damn it to hell! [L Am]
¡Qué alivio!	What a relief!
¡Qué barbaridad!	How terrible!
¡Qué bárbaro!	How terrible!
¡Qué cara!	What nerve!
¡Qué coñazo!	What a bitch of a problem! [Spain]
¡Qué cruz!	What a drag!
¡Qué disparate!	How absurd!
¡Qué emoción!	How exciting!
¡Qué gusto!	What a pleasure!
¡Qué lata!	What a drag! What a pain!

¡Qué locura!	This/That is nuts!
¡Qué mala onda!	How awful!
¡Qué mala pasada!	What a dirty trick!
¡Qué perra vida!	Life's a bitch!
¡Qué rico!	How delicious!
¡Qué tonterías!	What nonsense!
¡Qué va!	Come on!
¡Qué vaina!	Darn! What a pain! [most of C Am, Ven, Col]
¡Qui ubole!	Hi! [most of L Am]
¡Quieto!	Quiet! Pipe down!
¡Rápido!	Quick!
¡Rayos!	Blast!
¡Rin!/¡Riiiin!	Ring! (phone or doorbell)
¡Sal!	Get out!
¡Sal si puedes!	Save yourself!
¡Salud!	Cheers!
¡Shhh!	Shhh!
¡Simón!	Natch! Yeah!
¡Sin bromas!	No kidding!
¡Socorro!	Help!
¡Sooo!	Whoa! (to stop an animal)
¡Suácate!	Boom! Zap! [S Am]

¡Suerte!	Good luck!
¡Tanto mejor!	So much the better!
¡Tanto peor!	So much the worse!
¡Ten piedad!	Have mercy!
¡Toc toc!	Knock knock!
¡Toma!	So there!
¡Tranquilo(-a)!	Simmer down! Take it easy! Easy does it!
¡Uf!	Whew! (relief)
¡Úhule!	Yikes! [Mex]
¡Ups!	Oops!
¡Uuuh!	Boo!
¡Vale!	Right! Agreed! [Spain]
¡Vámonos!	Let's go!
¡Vaya!	Right! Agreed! [Mex, C Am, Col]
¡Vete!	Go away!
¡Viva...!	Hooray for ...! Long live ...!
¡Whoa!	Eeeek! Yikes! (unpleasant surprise)
¡Ya estamos!	We're done!
¡Ya mero!	Almost! [Mex]
¡Ya veremos!	We'll see!
¡Ya voy!	Coming!
¡Yupi!	Hooray!
¡Záfate!	Scram! Scat! [Mex, C Am]
¡Zas!	Presto! Zap!

Sir, bring another round of the same,
please.
Serve us the same thing.
Again, please.

I'm hungry!
Let's eat!
I'm starving!
I've got to eat something
to keep me on my feet.

No, thanks, I have to drive.
I don't drink much.
Just a little drop!
Just a little bit, thanks.

Something to drink, please!
Fill it up, please. Give me another one.
Can you bring me a drink?
I'm really thirsty!
A little drink to wet my whistle.

Go to hell!
Screw you!
Take this!

Have you lost your mind?
Are you crazy?
You've got a screw loose!
How crazy!
You're bonkers!

You're getting a smack in the kisser!
You asked for it!

You're gonna get a knuckle sandwich,
asshole!
Do you see this fist?

Excellent! I love it!
Super! Great!
Bravo! Well done!
Way to go!

I swear on my mother's grave!
I swear!
I give you my word of honor!

I've told you a thousand times …
Are you out of your mind?
You've gone bananas!

Enough already!
I've had enough!
I've had it up to here!
End of discussion!

It smells bad.
Something is rotten. It stinks.
What a terrible odor!

What stress!
More work? Help me!
What a difficult day!

Let me think about it for a minute.
On second thought, it's true …

I'm a zombie, completely beat.
I'm so sleepy I'm about to fall over.
I'm going to bed to get some shut-eye.
Good night!

We'll call each other, right?
If you don't catch me at home,
call me on my cell phone.
We'll be in touch.
You've got my e-mail address, right?

Quote ... unquote. (often ironic,
as in **mi "amigo"** to refer to
a person who is unfriendly)
You know what I'm trying to say.

Blah, blah, blah!
What a gab session!
They're talking a blue streak!

Shhh! Hush!
Silence!
Don't say a word.
It's a secret.
Remember: Mum's the word!

Do you realize what time it is?
What time is it?
I'm really behind schedule.
It's gotten late (on me).
Time flies.
See you later!

Give me 5 minutes.
Coming!
Wait for me!

Very expensive!
The price is sky high.
It costs an arm and a leg!

I don't have a plug nickel.
I don't have anything to my name.
I'm poor as a church mouse.
I'm flat broke. [parts of L Am, Spain; not Mex]

I'll drive.
Yes, by car.
I'm queen of the road!
When the traffic is light.

I'm going by plane.
As the crow flies.

I'm going on foot.
I'm a pedestrian.
I love going for walks.
Hoofing it.
A long walk—I love it!

I prefer to go riding.
Giddyup!
I'm going out the door.

Be careful!
Watch out!
Look at that!
Keep your eyes peeled!

I've got my fingers crossed.
Hang in there!
Good luck!
Hope so!
Hope everything works out well.

It's all over!
They're done for!
Done!
They went bankrupt! They're screwed.

Oh dear! What a problem!
Good Lord!
It's at fever pitch!

I don't know!
God knows!
Go figure.
I don't have the slightest idea.

I don't care!
I don't give a damn! [Mex, C Am]
I don't give a damn! [Spain]

What a scatterbrain!
It completely slipped my mind!

How stingy!
What a tightwad!
He's really stingy.

Calm down!
It's not all that bad.
Calm down.

So-so.
Okay.

Perfect!
Great!

No!
That's just not done.
Don't do that!

It's to die for!
(lit., It's finger-lickin' good!)
Delicious!

Drunk!
This guy is smashed!
He looks like a fumigated spider!
He'll have to sleep it off.

english-spanish index

affectionate *cariñoso(-a)* 41
la agencia de contactos (quiz) 132–33
aggressive *agresivo(-a)* 42
alert *despierto(-a)* 74
amusement *la diversión* 95
anger *la cólera* 96
annoyance (gestures) *el fastidio (ademanes)* 142
anxious *ansioso(-a)* 77
attitudes *las actitudes* 74–91, 95–117

bad reputation *la mala reputación* 85
body, parts of the *el cuerpo* 129
body language *el lenguaje corporal* 129
boring *aburrido(-a)* 43

calm *calmado(-a)* 76
character types *el carácter, tipos de* 2–37, 41–71
cheerful *alegre* 78
clumsy *torpe* 44
concentration *la concentración* 97
confrontation *el enfrentamiento* 134–35
contempt *el desprecio* 98
crafty *taimado(-a)* 45
crazy *loco(-a)* 46

decisive *decidido(-a)* 2
determination *la determinación* 99
disapproval *la desaprobación* 100
discouragement *el desánimo* 101
disorganized *desorganizado(-a)* 35
distracted *distraído(-a)* 9
distrustful *desconfiado(-a)* 47
dogmatic *dogmático(-a)* 48

eccentric *excéntrico(-a)* 49
embarrassment *la vergüenza* 102
emotions *las emociones* 74–91, 95–117

encouraging *alentador(a)* 80
enthusiastic *entusiasta* 4
erudite *erudito(-a)* 6

face *la cara* 125
facial descriptions *las caras, descripciones de* 120–33
facial types *las caras, tipos de* 126–28
fear *el miedo* 103
focused *concentrado(-a)* 8
food and drink (gestures) *la comida y la bebida (ademanes)* 140
friendly *amable* 82

generous *generoso(-a)* 10
gestures *los ademanes* 140–50
good reputation *la buena reputación* 84
gossipy *chismoso(-a)* 50
gratitude *la gratitud* 104

hair *el pelo* 120–24
happy *feliz* 86
health *la salud* 105
helpful *servicial* 12
honest *honesto(-a)* 51
hostile *hostil* 83
how do I look? *¿cómo me veo?* 130
Humorómetro (quiz) 92–94; results 118
hypocrisy *la hipocresía* 106
hypocritical *hipócrito(-a)* 52

ignorant *ignorante* 7
immature *inmaduro(-a)* 15
indecent *indecente* 53
indecisive *indeciso(-a)* 3
indifferent *indiferente* 13, 89
insignificant *insignificante* 54
inspiration *la inspiración* 107
insults (gestures) *los insultos (ademanes)* 141

interjections *las exclamaciones* 136–39
intermediary *el/la intermediario(-a)* 55

jealousy *los celos* 108
joy *el júbilo* 109

killjoy *el/la aguafiestas* 5
kindly *bondadoso(-a)* 56

laughter *la risa* 110
lazy *perezoso(-a)* 37
leader *el/la líder* 57
life of the party *el corazón del grupo* 58
loser *el/la perdedor(a)* 59

mature *maduro(-a)* 14
mean *malo(-a)* 19
melodramatic *melodramático(-a)* 60
mocking *burlón (burlona)* 81
modest *modesto(-a)* 16
money (gestures) *el dinero (ademanes)* 145
moods *los humores* 74–91, 95–117

nice *simpático(-a)* 18

obliging *complaciente* 61
optimistic *optimista* 20

passionate *apasionado(-a)* 88
peacemaker *el/la mediador(a)* 62
Personalidatos (quiz) 38–40; results 72
pessimistic *pesimista* 21
polite *cortés* 22
praise (gestures) *los elogios (ademanes)* 142
pretentious *pretensioso(-a)* 63
profound *profundo(-a)* 24
promises (gestures) *las promesas (ademanes)* 142
prosperous *próspero(-a)* 64

relaxed *relajado(-a)* 26
reliable *confiable* 65

relieved *aliviado(-a)* 90
reserved *reservado(-a)* 28
respectful *respetuoso(-a)* 66
romantic *romántico(-a)* 67
rude *descortés* 23

sad *triste* 79
satisfaction *la satisfacción* 111
self-confident *seguro(-a) de sí mismo(-a)* 30
senses, the (gestures) *los sentidos (ademanes)* 143
show-off *el fantoche* 17
sleep *el sueño* 112
sociable *sociable* 32
star *la estrella* 68
stiff *rígido(-a)* 27
stingy *tacaño(-a)* 11
suffering *el sufrimiento* 113
superficial *superficial* 25
surprise *la sorpresa* 114

talk (gestures) *la conversación (ademanes)* 144
talkative *hablador(a)* 29
time (gestures) *la hora (ademanes)* 145
tired *cansado(-a)* 75
touchiness *la susceptibilidad* 115
transportation (gestures) *el transporte (ademanes)* 146

uncertainty *la incertidumbre* 116
uncomfortable *incómodo(-a)* 69
unhappy *desdichado(-a)* 87
unsociable *poco sociable* 33
unsure of oneself *inseguro(-a) de sí mismo(-a)* 31

well-informed *informado(-a)* 70
well-organized *organizado(-a)* 34
wolf *el buitre* 71
wonder *el asombro* 117
workaholic *trabajólico(-a)* 36
worried *angustiado(-a)* 91

spanish-english index

aburrido(-a) *boring* 43

las actitudes *attitudes* 74–91, 95–117

los ademanes *gestures* 140–50

la agencia de contactos 132–33

agresivo(-a) *aggressive* 42

el/la aguafiestas *killjoy* 5

alegre *cheerful* 78

alentador(a) *encouraging* 80

aliviado(-a) *relieved* 90

amable *friendly* 82

angustiado(-a) *worried* 91

ansioso(-a) *anxious* 77

apasionado(-a) *passionate* 88

el asombro *wonder* 117

bondadoso(-a) *kindly* 56

la buena reputación *good reputation* 84

el buitre *wolf* 71

burlón (burlona) *mocking* 81

calmado(-a) *calm* 76

cansado(-a) *tired* 75

la cara *face* 125

el carácter, tipos de *character types* 2–37, 41–71

las caras, descripciones de *facial descriptions* 120–33

las caras, tipos de *facial types* 126–28

cariñoso(-a) *affectionate* 41

los celos *jealousy* 108

chismoso(-a) *gossipy* 50

la cólera *anger* 96

la comida y (la) bebida (ademanes) *food and drink (gestures)* 140

¿cómo me veo? *how do I look?* 130

complaciente *obliging* 61

la concentración *concentration* 97

concentrado(-a) *focused* 8

confiable *reliable* 65

la conversación (ademanes) *talk (gestures)* 144

el corazón del grupo *life of the party* 58

cortés *polite* 22

el cuerpo *body, parts of the* 129

decidido(-a) *decisive* 2

el desánimo *discouragement* 101

la desaprobación *disapproval* 100

desconfiado(-a) *distrustful* 47

descortés *rude* 23

desdichado(-a) *unhappy* 87

desorganizado(-a) *disorganized* 35

despierto(-a) *alert* 74

el desprecio *contempt* 98

la determinación *determination* 99

el dinero (ademanes) *money (gestures)* 145

distraído(-a) *distracted* 9

la diversión *amusement* 95

dogmático(-a) *dogmatic* 48

los elogios (ademanes) *praise (gestures)* 142

las emociones *emotions* 74–91, 95–117

el enfrentamiento *confrontation* 134–35

entusiasta *enthusiastic* 4

erudito(-a) *erudite* 6

la estrella *star* 68

excéntrico(-a) *eccentric* 49

las exclamaciones *interjections* 136–39

el fantoche *show-off* 17

el fastidio (ademanes) *annoyance (gestures)* 142

feliz *happy* 86

generoso(-a) *generous* 10

la gratitud *gratitude* 104

hablador(a) *talkative* 29

la hipocresía *hypocrisy* 106
    hipócrito(-a) *hypocritical* 52
    honesto(-a) *honest* 51

la hora (ademanes) *time (gestures)*
    145
    hostil *hostile* 83

los humores *moods* 74–91, 95–117
    Humorómetro 92–94; resultados
    118

ignorante *ignorant* 7

la incertidumbre *uncertainty* 116
    incómodo(-a) *uncomfortable* 69
    indecente *indecent* 53
    indeciso(-a) *indecisive* 3
    indiferente *indifferent* 13, 89
    informado(-a) *well-informed* 70
    inmaduro(-a) *immature* 15
    inseguro(-a) de sí mismo(-a)
      unsure of oneself 31
    insignificante *insignificant* 54

la inspiración *inspiration* 107

los insultos (ademanes) *insults*
    (gestures) 141

el/la intermediario(-a) *intermediary*
    55

el júbilo *joy* 109

el lenguaje corporal *body language*
    129

el/la líder *leader* 57
    loco(-a) *crazy* 46

maduro(-a) *mature* 14

la mala reputación *bad reputation*
    85
    malo(-a) *mean* 19

el/la mediador(a) *peacemaker* 62
    melodramático(-a) *melodramatic*
    60

el miedo *fear* 103
    modesto(-a) *modest* 16

optimista *optimistic* 20
    organizado(-a) *well-organized* 34

el pelo *hair* 120–24
el/la perdedor(a) *loser* 59
    perezoso(-a) *lazy* 37
    Personalidatos 38–40; resultados
    72
    pesimista *pessimistic* 21
    poco sociable *unsociable* 33
    pretensioso(-a) *pretentious* 63
    profundo(-a) *profound* 24

las promesas (ademanes) *promises*
    (gestures) 142
    próspero(-a) *prosperous* 64

relajado(-a) *relaxed* 26
    reservado(-a) *reserved* 28
    respetuoso(-a) *respectful* 66
    rígido(-a) *stiff* 27

la risa *laughter* 110
    romántico(-a) *romantic* 67

la salud *health* 105
la satisfacción *satisfaction* 111
    seguro(-a) de sí mismo(-a)
      self-confident 30

los sentidos (ademanes) *senses, the*
    (gestures) 143
    servicial *helpful* 12
    simpático(-a) *nice* 18
    sociable *sociable* 32

la sorpresa *surprise* 114
el sueño *sleep* 112
el sufrimiento *suffering* 113
    superficial *superficial* 25
la susceptibilidad *touchiness* 115

tacaño(-a) *stingy* 11
    taimado(-a) *crafty* 45
    torpe *clumsy* 44
    trabajólico(-a) *workaholic* 36
el transporte (ademanes)
      transportation (gestures) 146
    triste *sad* 79

la vergüenza *embarrassment* 102